BIBLE KEY WORDS

II. THE CHURCH

MANUALS FROM KITTEL

Translated and edited by
J. R. COATES

───

BIBLE KEY WORDS
FROM GERHARD KITTEL'S
*THEOLOGISCHES WÖRTERBUCH
ZUM NEUEN TESTAMENT*

THE CHURCH

BY

KARL LUDWIG SCHMIDT

LONDON
ADAM AND CHARLES BLACK
SOHO SQUARE

THIS EDITION FIRST PUBLISHED 1950
BY A. AND C. BLACK LIMITED
4, 5 AND 6 SOHO SQUARE LONDON W.1

Translated from the first
edition, Stuttgart, 1938,
and with additional notes
by J. R. Coates

MADE IN GREAT BRITAIN
PRINTED AT THE UNIVERSITY PRESS
ABERDEEN

PREFACE

AMONG the key words of the Bible, ἐκκλησία holds a place of special importance, indicating as it does the concrete phenomenon in which are seen those acts of the Creator which give meaning to history, the immediate objective for which Christ gave his life, and the organ of the Holy Spirit for the furthering of the Kingdom of God on earth.

" If the revelation of God in Christ is of supreme moment for mankind, the Christian community is also supremely significant. For the revelation occurred only within the life of that community. God did not manifest himself in Jesus alone, but in the life of the group which was formed about him and in whose creation he was himself the decisive factor. It was in Jesus *as known in the Church* that the fresh activity of God among men, which we call the revelation in Christ, occurred. And that revelation is not merely remembered in the Church ; it is constantly present wherever there is genuine Christian fellowship." (Prof. John Knox, Union Theol. Seminary, N.Y. : *The Christian Answer*, 1946, p. 242.)

The Church is the clue to the Bible as history, and it is also the culmination of the Bible as theology. Biblical theology is not one of a number of possible interpretations of the universe, provoking thought ; it is good news, a message and a call, an offer and an invitation, demanding action. The challenge of the Bible is not, " Do you agree ? " but " Do you believe ? " and " Will you join up ? " God is in Christ reconciling the world to himself, even through the Church, which is his body.

It might be said that the Church is both the theme of the Bible and its writer. Bible and Church explain each other, judge each other, need each other. Both are organs of the living God, and neither can function properly without the other. If the Church fails, it is because it is not Biblical enough, and if Bible study becomes pedantic and arid, it is because it is divorced from worship and service in the living fellowship of the Church.

In what sense did Christ found the Church? When did it actually come into existence? How are we to understand the Matthaean account of the incident at Caesarea Philippi? What was St. Paul's attitude towards the Church in Jerusalem? What is the relation between the Church and the Churches? What is implied in the expression, " the body of Christ " ? What does the Old Testament contribute to the Christian doctrine of the Church? Is the New Testament idea of the Church eschatological?

Prof. K. L. Schmidt has already done, and is still doing, much to help us to answer these and other questions concerning the Church. The present volume is a translation, slightly abridged, of his article on ἐκκλησία in the *Theological Dictionary of the New Testament*, begun by Gerhard Kittel, who died in 1948, and now under the editorship of Gerhard Friedrich. It first appeared in 1936, and its value is recognised by George Johnston, in his important book, *The Church in the New Testament* (1943), and by other British and American scholars, who have expressed their desire for an English version of it. My warmest thanks are due to the author for his friendly assistance. He assures me that he still maintains the theses here set forth and says there is a good account of recent discussion in a revised and enlarged translation of *Aspects Nouveau du Probleme de l'Eglise*, by F. M. Braun, O.P., under the title, *Neues Licht auf die Kirche, die protestantische Kirchendogmatik in ihrer neuesten Entfaltung* (Benziger, Einsiedeln/Köln, 1946).

At a time when the Church is widely and deeply concerned about its true nature and proper function, it will be well if Dr. K. L. Schmidt's arguments—with their practical implications—receive the most earnest consideration. They cannot fail to help theology to be Biblical, and may help the Church to be Christian.

BIOGRAPHICAL NOTE

Karl Ludwig Schmidt was born at Frankfurt a.M., 5th February, 1891 ; studied at Marburg and Berlin ; served in the 1914-1918 war ; became Privatdozent at Berlin, 1918, and Professor at Giessen 1921, Jena 1925, Bonn 1929. As a member of the Social Democratic Party, he was dismissed from his post in 1933, and became a Pastor in Switzerland. Since 1935 he has been Professor of New Testament Theology at Basle.

Dr. Schmidt wrote articles for *Die Religion in Geschichte und Gegenwart* and *Theologisches Wörterbuch zum Neuen Testament* ; founded and edited *Theologische Blätter*, 1922-1937 ; and has been editor of *Theologische Zeitung* since 1945. His other principal writings are as follows—

Der Rahmen der Geschichte Jesu, 1919.

Die Pfingsterzählung und das Pfingstereignis, 1919.

Die Stellung der Evangelien in der allgemeinen Literaturgeschichte, 1923.

Die Stellung des Apostels Paulus im Urchristentum, 1924.

Die Kirche des Urchristentums, 1927 ; 2nd ed., 1932.

Das Gegenüber von Kirche und Staat in der Gemeinde des Neuen Testaments, in *Theol. Blätt.*, 1937, Sp. 1-16.

Le problème du Christianisme primitif, 1938.

Die Polis in Kirche und Welt, 1940.

Ein Gang durch den Galaterbrief, 1942 ; 2nd ed., 1947.

Die Judenfrage in Lichte der Kap. 9-11 des Römerbriefes, 1943 ; 2nd ed., 1947.

Aus der Johannes-Apokalypse, 1944.

Kanonische und apokryphe Evangelien und Apostelgeschichten, 1944.

Die Verkündigung der Kirche an die Gemeinde, 1944.

Das Pneuma Hagion als Person und als Charisma, 1946.

Israels Stellung zu den Fremdlingen und Beisassen und Israels Wissen um seine Fremdling- und Beisassenschaft, in *Judaica*, 1946, pp. 269-296.

Die Natur- und Geisteskräfte im paulinischen Erkennen und Glauben, 1947.

Wesen und Aufgabe der Kirche in der Welt, 1947.

Homo imago Dei in Alten und Neuen Testament, 1948.

The proclamation of the Church to the Congregation, in *Scottish Journal of Theology*, September 1948.

J. R. Coates.

CONTENTS

BIBLIOGRAPHY

H. W. Beyer : " Die Kirche des Evangeliums und die loslösung des Katholizismus von ihr " in Der römische Katholizismus und das Evangelium, 1931.

C. G. Brandis : 'Εκκλησία in Pauly-Wissowa, V, 1905.

G. Gloege : Reich Gottes und Kirche im N.T., 1929.

K. Holl : Ges. Aufsätze zur Kirchengeschichte II, 44 ff., 1928.

G. Holstein : Die Grundlagen des evangelischen Kirchenrechts, 1928.

F. J. A. Hort : The Christian Ecclesia, 1897.

A. Juncker : Neue Kirchliche Zeitung, 126 ff., 180 ff., 1929.

F. Kattenbusch : " Der Quellort der Kirchenidee " in Festgabe für Harnack, 1921 ; " Die Vorzugsstellung des Petrus und der Charakter der Urgemeinde zu Jerusalem " in Festgabe für K. Müller, 1922.

W. Koester : Die Idee der Kirche beim Apostel Paulus, 1928.

L. Kösters (Catholic) : Die Kirche unseres Glaubens, 1935.

O. Linton (Swedish) : Das Problem der Urkirche in der neueren Forschung, 1932. Review by F. Kattenbusch in Theol. Stud. Krit., 97 ff., 1938.

E. Lohmeyer : Vom Begriff der religiösen Gemeinschaft, 1925.

W. Macholz : " Um die Kirche " in Theol. Blätt., 323 ff., 1928.

A. Médebielle : in Dictionnaire de la Bible, Suppl. II, 487 ff., 1934.

W. Michaelis : Täufer, Jesus, Urgemeinde, 1928.

E. Peterson : Die Kirche, 1929.

H. Schlier : " Zum Begriff der Kirche im Eph.", in Theol. Blätt., 12 ff., 1927.

K. L. Schmidt : Die Kirche des Urchristentums, 1932 ; " Das Kirchenproblem im Urchristentum " in Theol. Blätt., 293-302, 1927 ; art. in Forschungen und Fortschritte, 277 f., 1927.

F. Siegmund-Schultze (ed.) : Die Kirche im N.T. in ihrer Bedeutung für die Gegenwart, 1930.

H. E. WEBER : " Die Kirche im Lichte der Eschatologie " in Neue Kirchliche Zeitung, 299 ff., 1926.

H. D. WENDLAND : " Der christliche Begriff der Gemeinschaft " in Theol. Blätt., 129 ff., 1930 ; Die Eschatologie des Reiches Gottes bei Jesus, 1931.

[J. R. COATES : The Coming of the Church, 1929.

R. NEWTON FLEW : Jesus and His Church, 1938.

G. JOHNSTON : The Church in the New Testament, 1943.

T. M. LINDSAY : The Church and the Ministry in the Early Centuries, 1902.

A. LOISY : The Gospel and the Church, 1903.

T. W. MANSON : The Church's Ministry, 1948.

J. OMAN : The Church and the Divine Order, 1911.

C. A. A. SCOTT : The Fellowship of the Spirit, 1921.

B. H. STREETER : The Primitive Church, 1929.

A. M. RAMSEY : The Gospel and the Catholic Church, 1936.

C. E. RAVEN : The Gospel and the Church, 1939.]

DISCUSSIONS OF MATTHEW XVI, 17-19

R. BULTMANN : Z.N.W., 165 ff., 1919-1920.

A. DELL : Z.N.W., 1 ff., 1914.

H. DIECKMANN : Biblica, 189 ff., 1923.

S. EURINGER : A. Ehrhard Festgabe 141 ff., 1922.

K. G. GOETZ : Unters. z. N.T. XIII, 1927.

K. GUGGISBERG : Z. f. Kircheng., 276 ff., 1935.

TH. HERMANN : Th. Bl., 203 ff., 1926.

F. KATTENBUSCH : Th. St. Kr., 96-131, 1922.

G. KRÜGER : Th. Bl., 302 ff., 1927.

J. SICKENBERGER : Theol. Revue, 1 ff., 1920.

D. VÖLTER : Nieuw Theol. Tijdschr., 174 ff., 1921.

[F. H. CHASE : Hastings D. B. III, 758-760, 795 f.

S. SCHECHTER : J.Q.R., 428 f., 1900.]

Square brackets here, and elsewhere indicate additions by the translator.

I. PRELIMINARY

THE Greek dictionary gives two meanings to ἐκκλησία:
(1) " gathering of the people ", (2) " church " ;
and calls the former secular, the latter Biblical or
ecclesiastical. The last edition of " Liddell and
Scott " retains this division, but sub-divides the second
part, bringing in the Septuagint : (1) " ' assembly
duly summoned ', less general than σύλλογος ",
(2a) " in LXX ' the Jewish congregation ' ", (2b)
" in N.T. ' the Church as a body of Christians ' ".

N.T. lexicons follow suit, but make a further distinction : (a) the whole body of believers, (b) the
individual congregation, e.g. one meeting in a house.
The question arises as to which of these came first,
and different answers are given. Grimm-Thayer
puts the local Church first : " those who anywhere, in
city or village, constitute such a company and are
united into one body " ; and gives the second place to
" the whole body of Christians scattered throughout
the earth ". Preuschen-Bauer does the same, but the
Catholic Zorell reverses the order : first " the whole
body of those who belong to the religious society
founded by Christ ", and second, " any particular
Church, i.e. believers in Christ in any region or city,
under their own bishop ; almost identical with
diocese ". It is sometimes hard to decide which of
these meanings to give to ἐκκλησία, and the dictionaries
do not always agree.

The question is generally decided on denominational
rather than scientific grounds. Anglicans like to
speak of the ἐκκλησία as the one Church, " the body
of Christians ". Roman Catholics start from the
universal Church, and immediately quote Matt. xvi,

18,[1] going on to emphasise the authority of the bishop over the individual congregation. The orthodox Protestant puts the universal first, the liberal the local, a certain confusion being due perhaps to reaction against the hierarchy. The same thing is found in translations and commentaries. A notable exception is Cremer's Biblico-theological Dictionary of N.T. Greek, revised by Kögel (1923), which digs deeper, here as elsewhere, and thus reaches a better lexical conclusion. Here ἐκκλησία in the N.T. is the " redeemed community " (*Heilsgemeinde*), this view being based on the use of the word in the O.T. for the whole community of the people of Israel (*Gesamtheit der israelitischen Volksgemeinde*). Sometimes it means the whole Christian body, and sometimes the same N.T. redeemed community localised (*in lokaler Begrenzung*—a careful and well-chosen phrase). This dictionary further points out that it is not always possible to differentiate clearly between the two meanings. Reference may be made here to Zorell's remark that Acts ii, 47 ; v, 11 and other passages may be understood in either sense, in view of the fact that at the beginning the universal Church and the particular Church were one and the same.

The piling up of a great variety of equivalents for ἐκκλησία is shown to be undesirable primarily by the simple but determinative fact that the N.T. always uses the same word, while we commonly say " Church " in some places and " Congregation " in others. Another fundamental argument in favour of confining ourselves to one single rendering is the

---

[1] An exception is found in L. Kösters' article on " Church " in the second edition of Lexicon f. Theol. u. Kirche V, 968 ff. : " no doubt used at an early date by the Hellenists in Jerusalem for the gathering of the local Christian congregation, and then for the whole Christian community ".

fact that secular Greek writers use the same word as the Biblical writers, both O.T. and N.T. We must examine the question whether we could not, or should not, use either " Church " or " Congregation " uniformly in the N.T. Such an investigation will bring us face to face with the decisive questions concerning the Church in the N.T., viz., What is the relation between the so-called Church and the so-called Congregation ? Which of the two is intended at Matt. xvi, 18 ? Is the original company of Christians at Jerusalem Church or Congregation ? What is the connection between that original body and the other companies of Christians throughout the Roman Empire ? What exactly does ἐκκλησία mean to Peter's Jewish Christians, what to Paul's heathen converts, what to the Catholics of the ancient Church ? We ought indeed to go further, and inquire whether either " Church " or " Congregation " should not be adopted as the one and only rendering of ἐκκλησία throughout the whole Bible. This raises the whole question of the relation of the N.T. to the O.T. Just as a Hebrew expression lies behind the LXX ἐκκλησία,[1] so there is Aramaic, the language of Jesus and of the early Church in Jerusalem, behind

---

[1] E. Peterson, Die Kirche (1929), 19 : " It is not enough to derive the technical meaning of ἐκκλησία from the LXX ; it must rather be interpreted in the light of the new situation in which the apostles found themselves ". Certainly the LXX alone is not enough ; we must rather go back to the Hebrew text. Peterson considerably weakens his case by not troubling about either the Greek or the Hebrew O.T. His thesis, equating Church with Church of the Gentiles, comes to grief on the very fact that the same expression occurs in the LXX, and among Jewish and Gentile Christians. He does not feel the need to show how the same expression can mean different things.

[On LXX usage see further pp. 51 ff, and cf. J. Y. Campbell in Journal of Theol. Studies (1948), pp. 130-142, where he favours the translation, " meeting ".]

ἐκκλησία in the Gospel, and this has to be discovered. The search for it will be concerned with matters of fact.

Finally we ought to thrash out the question whether there is not one single rendering to be found, which could be used throughout the whole of Greek literature both sacred and profane. Could it be " assembly " or " gathering " ? This leads to the further question why the Christians of the N.T. avoided a term expressly connected with religion, and chose a thoroughly secular word.

The dictionaries show that in both religious and secular Greek ἐκκλησία covers the two ideas of coming together and being together, and this seems to point to some such rendering as " gathering ", which has the advantage of being available for the abstract as well as the concrete.

II. NEW TESTAMENT

THE word ἐκκλησία is not found in the following Books : Mark, Luke, John, II Tim., Titus, I Peter, II Peter, I John, II John, Jude.[1] Its absence from II Tim., Titus, I and II John is not surprising, since I Tim. and III John have it—and Jude is too short to be of statistical value. What is more remarkable is its non-appearance in the Petrine Epistles. But it may well be asked whether the thing itself is not there, although the word is missing, since in I Pet. special emphasis is laid upon the O.T. community and its meaning, with the use of O.T. expressions ;[2] and the same question forces itself upon our attention in the case of the three Gospels, Mark, Luke and John.

I. ACTS OF THE APOSTLES

Since the Matthaean ἐκκλησία passages are disputed and of doubtful interpretation, it seems better to start from the frequent and varied use of the word in Acts. The early examples are of the highest importance, viz., ii, 47 ;[3] v, 11 ; vii, 38 ; viii, 1 ; viii, 3 ; ix, 31. Here we read of " the ἐκκλησία which was in Jerusalem " (viii, 1) ; of Israel as " the ἐκκλησία in the wilderness " (vii, 38), echoing Deut. ix, 10, where LXX ἐκκλησία = Heb. qahal ; and of the ἐκκλησία " throughout all Judaea and Galilee and Samaria " (ix, 31).[4] While the individual congregation is

[1] I Pet. and II Pet. are overlooked in all editions of Cremer's N.T. Wörterbuch.
[2] [See E. G. Selwyn, I Peter, pp. 81-90.]
[3] [R.V. omits ἐκκλησία here, with many MSS.]
[4] " Throughout . . . Samaria " is probably to be taken

generally indicated, in one example the reference is
to a group of congregations, and therefore " Church "
is a better rendering than " Congregation ". It
should be added that there is some good textual
evidence for reading the Plural at ix, 31, instead of the
Singular,[1]—ἐκκλησία and ἐκκλησίαι both mean the
same thing. The Plural is better attested at xv, 41,
where only B D pc have the Singular, and is undisputed at xvi, 5. Elsewhere the Singular predominates
and indicates, either explicitly or by implication, the
congregation at Jerusalem (xi, 22 ; xii, 1—D pc " in
Judaea " ; xii, 5 ; xv, 4, 22) ; or at Syrian Antioch
(xi, 26 ; xiii, 1 ; xiv, 27 ; xv, 3) ; or at Caesarea
(xviii, 22) ; or at Ephesus (xx, 17, 28). The phrase
κατ᾽ ἐκκλησίαν (xiv, 23) means " Church-wise "
(*gemeinde-weise*) and may presuppose the Plural use
of the word ; Luther translates " *in den Gemeinden* " ;
A.V. and R.V. " in every Church ". A specially
pregnant saying is Acts xx, 28 ; Nestle compares this
with Ps. lxxiii, 2 (Heb. lxxiv, 2) where, however, the
word is συναγωγή (Heb. 'edhah).

The special peculiarity of the N.T. idea of the Church
comes out clearly in the passages just reviewed. It
must be emphasised that, without regard to any
question of precedence, the congregation at different
places is simply called ἐκκλησία. Mere localisation
is not the main point in these cases—as is shown by the
mention of an ἐκκλησία " throughout all Judaea
and Galilee and Samaria " (Acts ix, 31). It must

---

attributively with R.V., and not predicatively with A.V., the
omission of the second article being permissible in Hellenistic
Greek, though it is found at I Cor. i, 2 and II Cor. i, 1—and
is regarded as " better " Greek !

[1] Nestle unfortunately prints the Singular, without noting
the important Plural reading, while Bruder prints the Plural and
gives the Singular [as the reading of A B C etc.].

further be emphasised that Singular and Plural are used promiscuously. This does not mean that the ἐκκλησία is divided into ἐκκλησίαι, or that, *vice versa*, it is formed by the coming together of the latter. It means that *the* ἐκκλησία is present in a certain place, and this is not affected by the mention of ἐκκλησίαι elsewhere. When we translate, we must either say " Congregation " and " Congregations ", or " Church " and " Churches " ; and the former is to be preferred. The reason why we cannot entirely dispense with the word " Church " is that " Congregation " has come to be used to differentiate the smaller local group from the whole body of Christian people. It is significant that the same term is applied to the Jewish Christian Congregation, say, in Jerusalem, and to a Gentile Christian one, e.g. in Antioch. Ornamental epithets are never employed ; the only attribute, so to speak, is the Genitive, " of God ", which comes from the O.T. It is generally omitted, but always to be understood, in order to give ἐκκλησία its full weight. The ἐκκλησία of God is always regarded as being distinguished from, or opposed to, other forms of society—as is made clear at Acts ii, 47, where the Christians are distinguished from " all the people " (λαόν) or " all the world " (D reads κόσμον).

Three times in one chapter (xix, 32, 39, 40) ἐκκλησία means an assembly or gathering of the heathen, and is a purely secular expression. If we act on the fundamentally necessary and reasonable principle of consistency in translating passages from the same author, we shall have to reject the word " Church ". The word " Congregation " would be better, if we could use it, like the German " *Gemeinde* ", perhaps with a suitable adjective, to denote a political meeting. The simplest rendering is here the most satisfactory,

viz., " gathering ".[1] [If we were all Quakers, we
should have no hesitation in recommending " meeting "
as the English for ἐκκλησία in every context.   Cf. n. 1,
p. 3.]   This would give us the right starting-point
for differentiating between Church gatherings and
those of a worldly character.   It would then be easy
to see the obvious point implied by the use of both
Singular and Plural : if you speak of gatherings, you
must be thinking of people gathering themselves
together.   The mere gathering tells us nothing ;
everything depends on the character of those who are
gathered.   The addition of the words, " of God " or
" of the Lord ", points to him who gathers men, or
allows them to gather themselves ; and when this is
followed by the phrase, " which he purchased "
(Acts xx, 28), it is clear that God gathers his own.   The
ἐκκλησία is composed of *all* who belong to him.   The
use of the adjective " whole " at Acts v, 11 and xv,
22 bears out this idea of corporate unity ; it adds
nothing new, but serves to stress an idea already
involved in the expression, " Church of God ".   The
contrast with other (worldly) ἐκκλησίαι is not a
matter of quantity but of quality.   Size is an object
in the case of a national gathering, but not for the
gathering of the people of God.   The essential is that
God gathers his own.   Numbers depend upon him
who calls, and only secondarily upon those who
respond to the call.   " Where two or three are gathered
together in my name there am I in the midst of them."
(Matt. xviii, 20.)

[1] Nevertheless it cannot be suggested that we should abandon
the use of the word " Church " or the word " Congregation ".
Apart from the impossibility of such an undertaking, it is obviously
sensible to preserve the rich associations of such expressions.   But
it is desirable to establish the precise meaning of ἐκκλησία,
because this is a point at which linguistic accuracy makes a real
contribution to Biblical theology.

2. PAULINE EPISTLES I

Paul's usage is practically the same as that of Acts. There is no divergence between Jewish and Gentile Christians in their way of looking at this subject. The use of the Plural might be taken as showing that congregations stand side by side on an equal footing ; good examples of this are " other Churches " (II Cor. xi, 8) and " the rest of the Churches " (II Cor. xii, 13) ; cf. " no Church " (Phil. iv, 15). But that is not the decisive point ; it is not simply juxtaposition, but incorporation, with which we are concerned. The idea of corporate unity, mentioned above, finds expression in a number of ways : " the whole Church " (Rom. xvi, 23 ; I Cor. xiv, 23) ; " all the Churches " (Rom. xvi, 4, 16 ; I Cor. vii, 17 ; xiv, 33 ; II Cor. viii, 18 ; xi, 28) ; " everywhere in every Church " (I Cor. iv, 17).[1] Other references show that it is easy to pass from Singular to Plural, and *vice versa*. The alternative readings at I Cor. xiv, 35 show that. In any case the Plural is found in the two verses immediately preceding. Paul tells how he has persecuted the " Church " in Gal. i, 13 (cf. I Cor. xv, 9 ; Phil. iii, 6) and goes on in Gal. i, 22 to speak of the " Churches " of Judaea. Singular and Plural appear to be interchangeable in I Cor. x, 32 and xi, 16.

The ἐκκλησία is often definitely localised : Cenchreae (Rom. xvi, 1) ; Corinth (I Cor. i, 2 ; II Cor. i, 1) ; Laodicea (Col. iv, 16) ; Thessalonica (I Thess. i, 1 ; II Thess. i, 1) ; Asia (I Cor. xvi, 19) ; Galatia (I Cor. xvi, 1 ; Gal. i, 2); Macedonia (II Cor. viii, 1) ; Judaea (Gal. i, 22 ; I Thess. ii, 14).

The omission of the definite article is frequent, but makes no difference : I Cor. xiv, 4 (followed

---

[1] Paul loves such hyperbole, but has good ground for it.

immediately, in vv. 5, 12, by ἐκκλησία with the
Art.) ; xiv, 19, 28, 35 ; I Tim. iii, 5, 15. Obviously
'Εκκλησία has almost become a proper name. The
Article can also be omitted with the Plural, e.g.
II Cor. viii, 23, though it appears in vv. 19 and 24.[1]

A fellowship small enough to meet in a house can be
called ἐκκλησία, e.g., Rom. xvi, 5 ; Philem. 2. One such
finds a place beside the other larger Churches (I Cor.
xvi, 19), and it is important to notice that another is
included among the recipients of a profound discussion
of the true nature of the Church (Col. iv, 15).

Strong support is found in I Cor. i, 2 and II Cor. i, 1
for the contention that the Church is not a great community made up of an accumulation of small communities, but is truly present in its wholeness in every
company of believers, however small. The proper
translation in those verses is not " the Corinthian
Congregation "—taking its place beside the Roman,
etc.—but " the Congregation, Church, Gathering,
as it is in Corinth ". When it is said that in such a
gathering anyone is despised (I Cor. vi, 4), that
people come together (I Cor. xi, 18 ; cf. xiv, 23 and
Acts xiv, 27), that women must keep silence (I Cor.
xiv, 34), or that it must not be burdened (I Tim. v, 16),
it is not the local congregation, but the Church as a
whole, that is in view.

Practically the only attribute which Paul applies to
the ἐκκλησία by way of definition is the Genitive, " of
God ". He adds this both to the Singular (I Cor. i,
2 ; x, 32 ; xi, 22 ; xv, 9 ; Gal. i, 13 ; I Tim. iii, 5, 15)
and to the Plural (I Cor. xi, 16 ; I Thess. ii, 14 ; II
Thess. i, 4) ; that it is used with both is more important

---

[1] In the 6th ed. of Blass's N.T. Grammar, § 254, A. Debrunner
draws attention to the omission of the article with personal
designations like " God ", " Lord ", " dead ", " nations ".
It may be the same with ἐκκλησία.

than might appear at first sight. Distinguishing as we do between the Church as a whole and the individual congregation, we are accustomed to speak of " the Church of God ", but not of " the congregations of God ". The fact that Paul does so speak is another indication that he does not differentiate, as was done later, between " Church " and " congregation ". Again, if the words, " of God ", are omitted, as they often are, they are always to be understood, just as " Kingdom " in the N.T. always means the Kingdom of God, unless it is explicitly described as an earthly realm. It should be noted that in some MSS. they have suitably been added, e.g. at I Cor. xiv, 4 ; Phil. iii, 6. It is always God who works in and through the ἐκκλησία ; cf. I Cor. xii, 28.

God works " in Christ ", and so here and there the two names are both mentioned, the most perfect example being I Thess. ii, 14 : " the Churches of God which are in Judaea in Christ Jesus ". Gal. i, 22 has only " in Christ ", omitting " of God " ; Rom. xvi, 16 has only " of (the) Christ ", the Genitive having the same meaning as the formula " in Christ ".[1] In any case the Genitive τοῦ Χριστοῦ, should not be translated into the mere adjective, " Christian ". Paul is not speaking of a Christian Church or congregation, besides which there may be another Church or congregation, but of God's gathering in Christ. There is only one example of the addition of the words, " of the saints ", viz., I Cor. xiv, 33 (qualifying, as it happens, " all the Churches ") but this need cause no surprise, since at I Cor. i, 2

---

[1] Deissmann in his Paulus (1925), pp. 126 f. [pp. 93 f. in 1st ed.], rightly points to this interchange between the " in "-formula and the Genitive in many other passages, and suggests the phrase, *Genetivus communionis* or *mysticus*—which is open to criticism and at least superfluous.

the ἐκκλησία is identified with " them that are sanctified in Christ Jesus ".[1]

Before entering upon a discussion of the passages in Colossians and Ephesians, whose very richness and fulness have led some to deny their Pauline authorship, let us review those which have already been adduced, and compare them with the evidence of Acts. A thorough examination of the passages in which the word ἐκκλησία occurs in connection with the conflict between Paul and Jerusalem reveals a striking amount of agreement, from the statistical and lexicographical point of view. The relative frequency with which Paul adds the words, " of God ", brings him very close to the only instance in Acts, viz., xx, 28, where the quotation of Ps. lxxiv, 2 stresses a favourite idea of Paul's. So far as the actual words are concerned, Acts never connects the words, "Jesus Christ ", with ἐκκλησία, as Paul does.[2] But there is no real difference here ; it is merely a matter of expression. Paul elaborates that which he holds in common with the original disciples concerning the Church in the light of his practical experience. What distinguishes the " ἐκκλησία of God in Christ Jesus " is the fulfilment of O.T. prophecy in the New Covenant in the experience of a definite number of the disciples of Jesus, who have received special powers as witnesses of his resurrection. God's community of the New Covenant, first really in existence when Jesus Christ is risen from the dead, does not derive

[1] Cf. R. Asting, " Die Heiligkeit im Urchristentum " (Forschungen z. Rel. & Lit. d. A.T. & N.T., 1930) 134, 147, 204, 269.

[2] It may be remarked in passing that the bare simplicity of the ἐκκλησία sayings in Acts speaks for the high antiquity of the book. The obvious possibility that a later writer is reproducing very old sources without alteration does not apply in this case, for such a writer would be bound to introduce the richer language of his own age about the Church.

commission and claim from the enthusiasm of men of spiritual gifts, but only from a definite number of perfectly definite appearances of the risen Lord.[1] This is established, not only by Acts, which is open to question on many points, but above all by Paul's own statement in I Cor. xv, 3 ff., where the Apostle to the Gentiles attaches supreme importance to the alignment of his own experience on the Damascus road with the resurrection appearances to the original disciples. Paul himself was endowed with spiritual gifts, and knew what it was to have visions and auditions, trance and ecstasy (cf. II Cor. xii). But the source of his apostolate as service of God's ἐκκλησία did not lie in that quarter ; it was to be found simply and solely in the Damascus vision, the event which set him among the original witnesses of the resurrection.

From this point of view Paul is seen to have had the same view of the Church as the first Christians in Jerusalem.[2] Consistently with this, he recognised that the Jerusalem community and its leaders had special powers and privileges. It is impossible to exaggerate the importance of the collection which he made for the poor in Jerusalem—which was not so much for " the *poor* in Jerusalem " as for " the poor in *Jerusalem* ". Paul here recognised an obligation. It was not just a case of charity, though that came into it. Still less can it be called a piece of diplomacy on Paul's part. No : it shows a sense of duty on Paul's part, and of his respect for the men who first constituted God's ἐκκλησία in Christ. This respect was not based on personal grounds, as is shown by the fact that this same Paul

---

[1] K. Holl, following A. Schlatter, is specially emphatic on this point in his uncommonly helpful treatment of Paul's idea of the Church. See his Ges. Aufsätze z. Kirchengeschichte II (1928) 44 ff.

[2] Holl's conclusions are vitiated, in my judgment, by his failure to recognise this fact.

does not hesitate to speak ironically of " those who were reputed to be pillars ", and ultimately to accuse Peter of hypocrisy, when he stumbles in the matter of associating with Gentiles (Gal. ii). Yet Peter, entangled in sin as he is, remains for Paul the outstanding figure in the company of the faithful. It is not the individual so much as the community that is at stake—God's gathering in Christ. This " gathering " is not something to be dealt with by man's free will, or treated as an object of human speculation ; it is something ordained by God, utterly beyond our disposal. Psychologising value-judgments are of no avail in the case of a man far more highly endowed with the gifts of the Spirit than those who give him the appropriate label and then blame him for not breaking away from the primitive idea of the Church.[1]

Paul had recourse to a pattern whenever he spoke of the Church ; or rather, a pattern was given to him which he could neither disregard nor destroy. It was the Christians of Jerusalem who were in danger of destroying it, with their exaggerated idea of the importance of the original disciples as persons of authority and of Jerusalem as their holy place—their tendency, in a word, towards the rank theocracy against which all the prophets, from the great writing prophets to John the Baptist, and Jesus himself, had uttered warnings, never weary of drawing attention to the call of God to his people. Paul was in line with these, speaking more clearly than the original disciples of the ἐκκλησία in promise and fulfilment, and never dreaming of setting forth a new doctrine of the Church, opposed to that of Jerusalem. It was not he who was the innovator. The original disciples, who, of course, cannot be regarded as innovators, yet allowed innova-

---

[1] As H. Weinel does in the 1st ed. of Die Rel. in Gesch. u. Geg. III, 1130.

tions to become predominant. Paul agreed with those
among them who were true and had to be specially
on their guard at this point, that it is of the very essence
of the ἐκκλησία of God that its foundation and con-
tinuance are in its Messiah Jesus alone, and that its
Lord is Christ alone—not men in theocratic arrogance,
even though they have the gift of revelation to an
exceptional degree. It is possible that Paul had such
men in view when he added the words " in Christ
Jesus " or " of Christ ", to ἐκκλησία, and when he
said " the rock (πέτρα) was Christ " (I. Cor. x, 4).[1]

Paul, however, like Acts, gives no formal teaching
about the ἐκκλησία in these Epistles. What he talks
about is just the gathering of men as God's gathering in
Christ. The nature and significance of this are clear to
those who accept the fact of God's dealing with men,
and know how he does it in Christ, without the explicit
addition of attributes and predicates. An apparent exception to this is found in one passage only, viz., I Tim.
iii, 15, where the ἐκκλησία is characterised as " the
house of God ", with reference to " edification " (cf.
I Cor. xiv, 4 f., 12). But " house " is a colourless word,
when compared with ἐκκλησία ; and again everything
depends on what is conveyed by the words, " of God ".

3. PAULINE EPISTLES II : COLOSSIANS
AND EPHESIANS [2]

The doctrine of the ἐκκλησία receives its first explicit treatment in Colossians and Ephesians. The

---

[1] Cf. Lietzmann's footnote in Holl's Ges. Aufsätze II, 63 :
" May there not be a special point in saying that the rock was
Christ ? In any case for (Paul) himself obviously Christ is *the*
rock." Cf. also I Cor. iii, 11. We shall return to both these
passages when we deal with Matt. xvi, 18.

[2] Cf. N. Glubokowsky, W. F. Howard, K. L. Schmidt, " Christus
und die Kirche (Eph. v, 25-32) " in Theol. Blätt. (1930) 327 ff.

ἐκκλησία is the body of Christ (Col. i, 24), and Christ
is the head of this body (i, 18). It is the same in
Ephesians i, 22 and v, 23. The characteristic juxtaposition of Christ and the ἐκκλησία at Eph. iii, 21 and
v, 32 involves the ideas of co-ordination and sub-
ordination as expressed in Eph. v, 24, 25, 29 ; that ex-
plains the absence of " and " in many MSS. of iii, 21.
The holiness of the Church is only mentioned by Paul
at Eph. v, 27, though it is a commonplace among suc-
ceeding writers of the early period. Language of this
sort is excessive. Another example of it is found at
Eph. iii, 10, where we read of the manifold wisdom
of God being made known through the Church. It is
hard to be sure of the precise meaning of such statements in Ephesians ; the figurative language seems to
be employed without any logic. Christ is the ἐκκλησία
itself, since the latter is " the body of Christ ". But
then again he is also above the Church, being its head.
Such statements are closely inter-related. Christology
and ecclesiology are obviously on the same footing.
There is no obscurity for us here, so long as we read
simple words in a superficial way. But what the
apostle has in mind is a mystery, wrapped in obscurity,
around which the words of men revolve (Eph. iii, 4 f.).
This is no flight into the numinous. This is God's
revelation of the secret forever hidden from human
eyes. What goes on in the communion of Christ and
the ἐκκλησία is something conceived by God, created
by God, maintained by God. All culminates in the
final hymn (Eph. v, 25-32) : the familiar social code
simply means that the relation between man and wife
should be based on that between Christ and the
ἐκκλησία which in turn it illuminates.

The figures to which reference has just been
made have their origin in the language of contemporary mythology. It has been established by

H. Schlier [1] " that a consistent world of ideas finds expression in Ephesians, the author of which speaks the
language of a particular Gnostic circle. The redeemer,
who ascends to heaven, overcomes the heavenly powers
(Eph. iv, 8 ff.) on his way, and breaks through the wall
which divides the world from the divine kingdom
(ii, 14 ff.). He thus returns to himself, as to the higher
man (iv, 13 ff.), who lives his independent life in the
heavenly kingdom. He is, however, the head of the
body. In this he raises his members ($\mu\epsilon\lambda\eta$), creates
the ' new man ' (ii, 15), and builds his body up into the
heavenly building of his $\epsilon\kappa\kappa\lambda\eta\sigma\iota\alpha$ (ii, 19 ff. ; iv, 12 ff.,
16), in which God's work is made manifest (iii, 10 f.).
The saviour loves and cares for his Church, cleansing
and saving it. She is his wife and he her husband ;
they are bound to each other in obedience and love
(v. 22-32)."

There are six separate points here, each obviously
corresponding in only a limited way to the generally
accepted Christian affirmations, viz. (1) the redeemer's
ascension ; (2) the heavenly wall ; (3) the heavenly
man ; (4) the Church as Christ's body ; (5) Christ's
body as a heavenly building ; (6) the heavenly
marriage. The view repeatedly emphasised, that the
Church is the body of Christ, can scarcely be held
to involve the transfer of the relationship in anything
like a physical sense. The body of which Ephesians
speaks is, strictly, only a torso. But it grows up in all
things into the head, from which, on the other hand,
all growth proceeds. On the one hand Christ is the

---

[1] " Zum Begriff der Kirche im Eph." in Theol. Blätt. (1927)
12 ff. ; " Christus und die Kirche im Eph " (1930). The Mandaean Liturgies speak of a heavenly building, which is the great
place of light and also the $\overset{\text{\'}}{\alpha}\nu\theta\rho\omega\pi\sigma$, the $\overset{\text{\`}}{\alpha}\nu\eta\rho$ $\tau\epsilon\lambda\epsilon\iota\sigma$, the
$\overset{\text{\'}}{\alpha}\nu\theta\rho\omega\pi\sigma$ alternating with his $\sigma\hat{\omega}\mu\alpha$. See Lidzbarski, Man-
daean Liturgies (1920).

head, and on the other he is the whole body—including
the head.   This complicated theory can hardly be
regarded as a development of the Pauline teaching
in Rom. xii, 4 ff. and I Cor. xii, 12 ff.   Above all, the
equating of body, flesh, wife, church, cannot be
derived from Paul's way of putting things in his other
writings.   I Cor. xii is concerned with the relation of
Christians to one another, whereas in Ephesians they
are the body of Christ.   This world of ideas is more or
less clearly presented in the Valentinian Gnosis, the
Odes of Solomon, etc. :[1] the redeemer brings the
redeemed on high as his body ; Christ is the man whose
body the faithful are, and he himself is the head ; the
ἐκκλησία as the body of the man first comes into
existence through him and in him ; the Church is on the
one hand identical with the body of the man, or with
the man himself, but on the other hand his feminine

---

[1] E.g., Theodotus, the Valentinian Gnostic, says, ὁ μέγας
ἀγωνιστὴς Ἰησοῦς ἐν ἑαυτῷ δυνάμει τὴν ἐκκλησίαν ἀναλαβών
τὸ ἐκλεκτὸν καὶ τὸ κλητόν . . . ἀνέσωσεν καὶ ἀνήνεγκεν ἅπερ
ἀνέλαβεν (Clem. Al., Exc. Theod. lviii, 1).   The idea that the
faithful form the body of the heavenly man may be illustrated from
the Odes of Solomon xviii, 14 ff. : " They received my blessing and
lived ; and they were gathered to me and were saved ; because they
were to me as my own members and I was their head.   Glory to
thee our head, the Lord Messiah."   [Translated by Rendel
Harris.]   Schlier gives many other examples from Christian
apocryphal, Gnostic and Mandaean writings.   It is impossible to
deny the connection of all this with our subject, even though
details remain debatable.   It would be a mistake to regard this
way of looking at the matter as tantamount to handing Paul over
to the Gnostics.   Perhaps Schlier should have it made clearer
that in Ephesians, as elsewhere in the N.T., the Christological
language is polemical, being the first effective means of establishing
the unique worth of Jesus Christ, who remains the subject,
whatever new predicates are introduced.   The same applies to
the predicates " Lord " and " Saviour " and, above all, " Word ".
The point is not that Christ is the *Word*, but that *Christ* is the Word.
See the next two notes.

counterpart, generally called wisdom, sometimes takes his place. It is from this figure of marriage that we are to understand the remarkable words of Eph. v, 25-32, culminating in the affirmation that Christ nourishes and cherishes the Church.

A statement so elaborate and sublime conveys the impression that it must be the outcome of speculations in which the acknowledgment of God and his ἐκκλησία in Christ is largely determined by the pattern upon which it is superimposed. But such an impression must be firmly resisted. The treatment of wisdom has nothing to do with abstract speculation or esoteric knowledge. Similarly in Ephesians wisdom and the knowledge of God are not theoretical but practical, meaning the knowledge of the heart (i, 18), which is attained through obedience towards God—in a word, through faith.[1]

The discovery of the source from which Ephesians draws its ideology does not bring us to the end of our investigation ; we have still to ask why it was employed and to what end it was directed. Two closely related reasons may be suggested. (a) Gnostic ideology and vocabulary, as used in Ephesians, are well adapted to the purpose of setting forth the intimate relationship of Christ and Church, and are therefore brought into the service of a Christological ecclesiology. (b) Gnosticism provides a suitable background for the establishment of the high Christology which was necessary for dealing with the assault of false teaching and

[1] This may serve to correct Schlier's impression that in Die Kirche des Urchristentums, pp. 313, 315, I have failed to recognise " that the mythology of Ephesians is not used in the conventional way, viz., in the service of speculation ". In any case I entirely agree with him when he says that the mythology of Ephesians is the one medium through which the author and his hearers are able to understand one another. On p. 315 of my book I was only speaking of the limits of speculation concerning the Church.

the conflict between Jewish and Gentile Christians.
All the same, Ephesians is in fact thoroughly Pauline—
whether it was written by the apostle or by one of
his disciples. All kinds of difficulty beset an apostle
in those days, when he tried to explain the ἐκκλησία
of God in Christ, and when these are understood, it is
impossible to share the widespread critical certainty
that Paul could not have been the author of (Colossians
and) Ephesians. Paul had to fight against Jewish
Christians or Jews at one extreme, and Gentile Christians or Gnostics at the other, the former not going far
enough and the latter going too far. His language had
to be strong and elevated, as it is in Ephesians. This
was a struggle within the Christian community, which
was always in danger of destroying the ideal of the
ἐκκλησία. The Church that is from above must be
set over against the Jewish claim for a privileged
position, the movement towards giving central authority
to certain men and one place, which was threatening
to lead the original disciples astray. Bizarre Gnostic
speculation about the marriage of Christ, as the male
principle, with wisdom as the female, must be countered
with the doctrine of the ἐκκλησία, which alone takes
the place of the " female ". The Paul whom we know
in the undisputed Epistles is quite at home in this kind
of disputing. That last point, about the " female ",
reminds us of II Cor. xi, 2, where Paul refers to his
effort to espouse the Corinthian Church to one husband,
to present it as a pure virgin to Christ. It has already
been pointed out that Rom. xii, 4 ff. and I Cor. xii,
12 ff. show Christians in relation to one another as
members of one body, and not in relation to Christ ;
but this is only a formal contrast, like that between
love to God and love to neighbour. The difficulty of
attributing to Paul what is said about the Church in
Colossians and Ephesians is not in the matter but in

the form ; it is easy to understand the substance of it coming from him, to meet a controversial situation of a special character, but it is far from easy to accept the assumption that he could ever have made such free use of the vocabulary of this Gnostic mythology.[1]

At any rate the point is pretty clearly made that the ἐκκλησία as the body of Christ is not a mere fellowship of men. The true meaning of the gathering of God in Christ can never be understood from the standpoint of social science. The one essential is communion with Christ. To put the matter in a nutshell—a single individual could be—would have to be—the ἐκκλησία if he has communion with Christ. This is the basis of true human brotherhood.[2] Over against all sociological attempts to comprehend the Church, it must be noted that for Paul, for those who followed him, and for the Fourth Evangelist, ecclesiology and Christology are identical. Paul says very emphatically that among Christians—in the ἐκκλησία as the body of Christ— all human divisions disappear (Col. iii, 11 ; Gal. iii, 28). The next verse in Galatians says, " and if ye

[1] The much discussed question of authenticity finds its crux here, regard being had also to the peculiar relationship between Colossians and Ephesians. There are traditionalist theologians who hold Ephesians to be genuinely Pauline, crediting the apostle with development, perhaps even to the length of Gnostic ways of thinking. In this connection T. Schmidt, in his Der Leib Christi Σῶμα Χριστοῦ (1919) goes so far as to assert that " in fact, nowhere else does Paul rise to the height of such a comprehensive view of the world and of history, embracing heaven and earth, past, present, and future ". On the other hand there are critical theologians who are led, by the fact that Gnostic language is used without the adoption of Gnostic ways of thought, to deny the Pauline authorship of Ephesians, while holding fast to its Pauline character.

[2] This is well shown in a lecture by the old-Catholic theologian, E. Gaugler, " Die Kirche, ihr Wesen und ihre Bestimmung " (Internat. Kirchl. Zeitschr. (1927), pp. 136 ff., esp. 146).

3

are Christ's, then are ye Abraham's seed, heirs according to promise ". If we understand Paul aright, we
must speak of the body of Christ with reserve. From
Paul's time onwards one dared not speak too loud, or
too much, of the organism which the body of Christ
had to represent. It was necessary to refrain from
an excessive use of figurative language, in order to
avoid the possibility of giving a wrong impression by
suggesting that the higher growth under discussion
was a natural growth. To be God's organ [discharging
a function of the divine life], means to give heed to
God's call. There can be no such thing as an unrelated
Christology or ecclesiology, in the sense of a Christ- or
Church-mysticism, since the God who speaks in Christ
is the God of the old covenant, who then institutes
the new covenant, and the gathering of God in Christ is
none other than the fulfilment of the O.T. gathering
of God. The same God has spoken and is speaking to
Israel with the word of promise, and to Christians with
the word of the fulfilment of this promise. Along with
the so-called Christ-mysticism and Christ-cult there
remain the God of the O.T. and his worshipping
community. When holiness is ascribed to the ἐκκλησία
that does not mean that she possesses it as a quality.
In other words, the true conception of church, congregation, God's gathering in Christ, is bound up with
a true conception of justification. That is what Paul
is always fighting for, whether against Jews or Gnostics.

4. The few instances of ἐκκλησία in the rest of the
N.T. add nothing new to what has been said above.
It only occurs in the framework of the Apocalypse :
thirteen times in the Plural and seven times in the
Singular, referring to the Churches at Ephesus,
Smyrna, Pergamum, Thyatira, Sardis, Philadelphia and
Laodicea. III John has the word three times, twice

with the Article and once without, though this makes
no difference. James v, 14, speaking of elders of the
ἐκκλησία, does not refer to a particular congregation, but
to the Christian community as a whole, to which the
Epistle is addressed. Heb. ii, 12 is a quotation of Ps.
xxii, 22, ἐκκλησία representing the Hebrew *qahal*. Heb.
xii, 23 is the only passage in which ἐκκλησία denotes
the heavenly Jerusalem, and it may be questioned
whether it is used here in its technical N.T. sense,
especially as it is coupled with πανήγυρις [which
Moffatt rightly translates " festal gathering ".][1]

---

[1] H. Windisch in his commentary rightly avoids " Gemeinde "
and translates " Festschar und Versammlung ".

III. GREEK USAGE

THE N.T. itself shows that ἐκκλησία is used in secular Greek for a gathering of the people (Acts xix, 32, 39 f.). The Biblical connotation is indicated by the addition of the words " of God ", with the further addition of " in Christ Jesus " in the N.T., whether expressed or understood. What is the significance of the fact that Greek-speaking Jews and early Christians chose this particular expression ? Could it already have been employed among the Greeks in a religious connection ?

From the time of Thucydides, Plato and Xenophon onwards, and then specially in inscriptions, ἐκκλησία is the gathering of the δῆμος in Athens and most Greek cities. The derivation is simple and significant : the assembled citizens are the ἔκκλητοι (called out), i.e. those who have been summoned by the herald.[1] This naturally suggests that in the Bible the reference is to God in Christ calling men out of the world.[2]

It is questionable whether ἐκκλησία ever meant a religious society in ordinary Greek.[3] If it did, we could well understand its appropriation by a Christian congregation. This would apply specially to Corinth, as pictured by Paul in I Cor. But, apart from the fact

[1] W. Koester, in " Die Idee der Kirche beim Apostel Paulus " (N.T. Abhandlungen xiv, 1—1928) follows others in referring to the form ἐκλησία which is not included even in the latest dictionaries. It would imply derivation from ἐκ-λαός, but it is so rare that no conclusions can be based on it.

[2] Cf. Deissmann, Light from the Ancient East, 112-114.

[3] Johannes Weiss believes it did (I Cor. p. xvii), relying on W. Liebenam, Zur Geschichte und Organisation des Römischen Vereinslebens (1890) ; E. Ziebarth, Das griechische Verein-swesen (1896)—though he gives no evidence for the word ἐκκλησία ;

that the evidence is too slight, Paul would never have
used a word with such associations, feeling as he did
that everything depended on God's gathering in
Christ. Some Gentile Christian circles, unfamiliar
with the LXX, may have thought of their fellowship
in terms of the derivation of ἐκκλησία, or as a kind of
club. It is altogether possible, indeed quite obvious,
that Christian congregations would copy contemporary
clubs in many matters of organisation.[1]

It was the Septuagint which really gave the word
ἐκκλησία to the N.T., after it had acquired its
specific value. As soon as converted Jews saw the
connection between the O.T. ἐκκλησία and that of the
N.T., it became regulative. The political assembly
of the ancient Greeks corresponds to this in a formal
way, but really only provides an analogy, neither more
nor less [2] ; just as the application, for polemical
purposes, of the title " Lord ", to Caesar is to be seen

and F. Poland, Geschichte des griechischen Vereinswesens (1909).
This evidence is not given in modern dictionaries like Preuschen-
Bauer and Moulton & Milligan. Lietzmann says expressly
(Cor., p. 4) that the word ἐκκλησία " does not appear as the
designation of a religious brotherhood ; the three apparent
exceptions prove this (Poland 332), since they use ἐκκλησία to
denote, not the brotherhood, but its gathering for business".

[1] Cf. G. Heinrici, " Zum genossenschaftlichen Charakter der
paulinischen Christengemeinden " in Theol. Stud. Krit. (1881)
505 ff. Against this it is justly urged that the matters involved
are common to the formation of all fellowships, and are not
peculiar to that age. For further detail see Johannes Weiss,
I Cor., pp. xx ff.

[2] E. Peterson goes further than this in Die Kirche, p. 19, n.
19 : " It can be shown in a number of ways that the λαός of the
Christian ἐκκλησία is a copy of the ancient δῆμος. I am not
only thinking of the forms of acclamation which passed over from
the δῆμος to the λαός, but would draw attention to J. Partsch's
discovery that the form in which the liberation of slaves was
proclaimed in the Christian ἐκκλησία goes back to a custom of the
secular ἐκκλησία (Sitzungsber. Heidelb. Akad. (1916) 44 f.)." The
connection may be rightly recognised in a single instance of this

as corresponding to the application of the same title to
Christ, but not as its prototype. This view is not
affected by the fact that the political assembly—at
least in classical times—was not without a religious
undertone, being regarded as one of the most important duties required by the gods when they founded
the city. That this was so may be seen from the prayers
which were customarily offered by the herald before
the ἐκκλησία and then by each speaker before he
made his speech.[1] The later adoption of secular
practices by the ancient Church is an entirely different
thing, and belongs to the history of the Church in Rome
and Byzantium.

That the Greek expression ἐκκλησία, in the sense
indicated, did become regulative, follows from the fact
that it held the field as the only technical term for the
Christian community. It was hardly necessary, even
if it had been possible, to translate ἐκκλησία into
Latin. Tertullian, who played so important a part
in the formation of ecclesiastical Latin, says *curia* in his

sort, but that does not prove the truth of Peterson's thesis that the
Christian ἐκκλησία was derived from that of the heathen. He
writes rather more cautiously on pp. 14 f., in words that should
be taken as a note with the passage already quoted : " The
secular ἐκκλησία of antiquity is a recognised institution
of the πόλις. It is the assembly of those who have full citizenship, met together for the performance of legal acts. Analogously
the Christian ἐκκλησία might be described as the assembly
of those who have full citizenship in the heavenly city, met together for the performance of prescribed acts of worship. . . . The
public and legal character of Divine Service in the Christian
Church shows that the Church owes much more to political
models, like the kingdom and the city, than to voluntary fellowships and societies."

[1] Cf. G. Busolt-H. Swoboda, Griechische Staatskunde I (1920),
518 f. ; II (1926), 996. Evidence for prayer in the Athenian
ἐκκλησία is found in Aristophanes, Equites, 763 ff. ; Demosthenes,
Or. xviii, 1 ; Plutarch, Pericles 8 (I, 156) ; Praecepta Ger.
Reipub. 8 (II, 803 f.) (Kleinknecht).

Apologeticum (39 end), and this is a perfectly sound translation of the Greek word ; but it did not become a technical term.[1] The same is true of Augustine's *civitas Dei*.[2] Among other renderings found here and there are *contio* and *comitia*.[3] *Convocatio* might have been adopted as a literal translation. But not one of these established itself as connoting the Church. The Romance-speaking peoples have followed the example of Rome, and modern Greeks have naturally kept the old term. The word " Church " almost certainly comes from the adjective κυριακός (of the Lord), but a kind of popular etymology connects it with ἐκκλησία. Why is that ? Why did the Greek word persist ? Perhaps it was felt in non-Christian circles that there was no Latin word exactly corresponding.[4] The matter was not decided by interesting and attractive analogies, but by the geneological descent of ἐκκλησία from the Greek Bible. The same term was retained, as κύριος was for " Lord ". The considerations here submitted do not constitute a mathematical demonstration that the LXX is entirely responsible ; but probably it was felt that what was required was more than just the word used by Greek-speaking Christians ; it must be a word hallowed by use in the holy Book.

[1] Cf. Harnack, Mission u. Ausbreitung I (1924), 420, n. 1. [See p. 30, n. 2. Ref. to Tertullian not in English trans., Mission and Expansion (1908) I, 407, n. 3.]

[2] F. Kattenbusch, in Der Quellort der Kirchenidee (Harnack-Festgabe (1921), pp. 142-172) says this is the first attempt to give a translation denoting the actual meaning of the word. On the other hand Kleinknecht says that " Civitas dei in Augustine gives the political idea of πολιτεία, under Platonic influence, in all its ancient many-sidedness, but certainly not that of ἐκκλησία ".

[3] Cf. Deissmann, Light from the Ancient East, 112-114.

[4] Deissmann recalls Pliny's letter to Trajan X, 110 (111), where the Latinised *ecclesia* occurs ; and a bilingual inscription at Ephesus, of A.D. 103-4, in which the Greek word ἐκκλησία is simply transcribed.

At the same time, this very word ἐκκλησία, with
its natural worldly associations, voices the greatest
claim of the Christian community over against the
world. Many Gentile Christians, like those who to-day
write the history of religion, thought of themselves as an
association for the worship of Christ, and might have
given themselves some kind of cultic title. There
were plenty to choose from, among contemporary
religious clubs and societies.

Heathen writers did actually apply such labels to the
Christian community. Lucian evidently regards it as
a θίασος [a religious guild or brotherhood like that of
the worshippers of Bacchus], when he calls the leader
θιασάρχης.[1] Celsus calls Christ's disciples θιασῶται.[2]
What is more striking is that Eusebius also twice calls
Christians θιασῶται, and once even applies the term
θίασος to the Church.[3] This is all the material of
this sort that is known, and the greatest care must be
taken to avoid the exaggeration of assuming that
Christianity was just one among other religious brotherhoods.[4] In order rightly to assess the juxtaposition

[1] Lucian, De Per. Morte, 11 : τὴν θαυμαστὴν σοφίαν τῶν
Χριστιανῶν ἐξέμαθε . . . προφήτης καὶ θιασάρχης καὶ συνα-
γωγεύς.

[2] Origen, Celsus iii, 23 : ὁ δὲ ἡμέτερος Ἰησοῦς ὀφθεὶς τοῖς
ἰδίοις θιασώταις—χρήσομαι γὰρ τῷ παρὰ Κέλσῳ ὀνόματι—ὤφθη
μὲν κατ᾽ ἀλήθειαν.
Origen is evidently astonished that Celsus should have employed
this expression. Similarly, in the Latin Church, in Minucius
Felix, Octavius, 8 f. (Migne P.L. III), a heathen speaks of the
Christian community as a *factio, coitio, consensio*—somewhat
derogatory words. See p. 30, n. 2.

[3] Eusebius, Hist. Eccl. I, iii, 12 : (Χριστὸς) αὐτὰς γυμνὰς ἀρετὰς
καὶ βίον οὐράνιον αὐτοῖς ἀληθείας δόγμασιν τοῖς θιασώταις
παραδούς. Cf. I, iii, 19. The word θίασος stands for Church
at X, i, 8.

[4] A striking example of such exaggeration and mistake occurs
in Der römische Staat und die allgemeine Kirche bis auf Dio-
cletian (1890), pp. 46 f. where the author, K. J. Neumann, asserts

of θίασος and ἐκκλησία, it must be remembered that
words denoting the various brotherhoods of the ancient
world were used with remarkable frequency, viz.,
θίασος, ἔρανος, κοινόν, σύνοδος, σύλλογος and many
others. None of these were appropriated by the
Christians. Further, although the names of individuals
were often derived from those of gods or other persons,
no such thing ever happened in the case of the name of
Jesus.[1] The name " Christians " is rarely found in the
N.T. (only Acts xi, 26 ; xxvi, 28 ; I Pet. iv, 16) ;
it became popular gradually at first, and in the form
" Chrestians " was connected with the proper name
" Chrestos ". Christians are partisans of Christ,
as Herodians, for example, are partisans of Herod
(Mark iii, 6 ; xii, 13 ; Matt. xxii, 16), supporters of one
particular movement among many.

The uniqueness of Christianity is much better
brought out by emphasising the ἐκκλησία (of God)
than by the choice of some cultic word, perhaps distinguished by the addition of a personal name. The
so-called Christ-cult was not, and did not wish to be,
one cult among others, but took its stand against all
cults, in the sense that it stood over against the whole
world, including the whole of the so-called religious
world. All that is guaranteed by the choice of the
designation ἐκκλησία, with which the words " of God "
are always to be understood.

The question may be asked, and has been asked,
who was the first within the Christian movement to
say ἐκκλησία ? Could it have been Paul who set the
fashion among Greek-speaking Christians ?[2] But it

that " it would actually have needed explaining, if Greek
Christians had not seen their new associations as religious brother-
hoods and *thiasoi* ". The presumable *abusus* on the part of certain
Gentile Christians, is, however, no *usus legitimus*.

[1] See the careful investigations of F. Poland (op. cit.).

[2] Kattenbusch (op. cit., p. 144, n. 1) is inclined towards this

seems difficult in this case to make any particular
individual responsible. It is more likely that the
expression arose among Greek-speaking Jewish Christians and their Gentile adherents, who formed congregations resembling the Hellenistic synagogues before
Paul's time.[1] As Jews, these Hellenistic Christians
were brought up on the LXX. They no longer
called themselves συναγωγή (about which more will
be said later) but ἐκκλησία. As Christians, they
seized upon the expression which was falling into
disuse among the Jews, who were tending more and
more to depart from LXX usage and confine συναγωγή
to its local meaning. That in itself made ἐκκλησία
preferable. The latter was also a more impressive
Greek word.[2] It should also be noticed that in the
LXX ἐκκλησία is made to stand out by the use of
laudatory epithets.[3]

view. Cf. F. Torm, Hermeneutik des N.T. (1930), p. 80. H.
Dieckmann's thesis, in De Ecclesia I (1925), p. 280 : " Nomen
Ecclesiae ad ipsum Christum ut auctorem reducitur " is also
rejected by Catholic scholars, on the ground that Jesus would
hardly have used Greek ; cf. K. Pieper, Jesus und die Kirche
(1932), p. 11.

[1] Cf. K. L. Schmidt, Die Stellung des Apostels Paulus im
Urchristentum (1924), p. 16.

[2] Wellhausen, on Matt. xvi, 18, expresses the opinion that " in
Greek ἐκκλησία is the more honourable word ". The passage
from Tertullian, Apologeticum 39, mentioned above, should be
understood as an emphatic paraphrase of the emphatic word
ἐκκλησία : " Hoc sumus congregati quod et dispersi, hoc
universi quod et singuli . . . cum probi, cum boni coëunt, cum
pii, cum casti congregrantur, non est factio dicenda, sed curia ".
Augustine's exposition of Ps. lxxxii, 1 is relevant here : he
says that convocatio (ἐκκλησία) is the word for the Christian
congregation and congregatio (συναγωγή) for the Jewish, because
the former is a nobler expression, meaning the calling together
of men, whereas the latter indicates the driving together of cattle.
See also Trench sub. voc. [and Schürer, G. J. V. 4th ed., II,
504 f.].

[3] Pointed out by Lietzmann on I Cor, i, 1 ; also by K. Pieper,

Why did the LXX translators almost always choose
ἐκκλησία to represent the Hebrew *qahal* ?   Quite apart
from the fact that the verbal root in both cases has
the same meaning, there is much to be said for the
conjecture that the choice was influenced by the simi-
larity of sound between the two words.[1]   This is
supported by the fact that Greek- and Latin-speaking
Jews were fond of adding Greek and Latin names
similar in sound to their Hebrew or Aramaic ones.[2]

op. cit., 20, and Harnack, Mission and Expansion, etc., I, 407,
where, however, the suggestion that the choice of the word
ἐκκλησία was a master-stroke is questionable, if not actually
misleading.

[1] As with ἀκροβυστία [and perhaps ἀγάπη and ὅσιοι, the
latter suggested by L. W. Grensted (see C. H. Dodd, The Bible and
the Greeks, p. 64, n. 1)].   Cf. Cremer-Kögel s.v. p. 566 and G.
Stählin, Skandalon, p. 44.

[2] The best-known example is Saul-Paul ; cf. Jesus-Jason, Silas-
Silvanus (Aram. *Shᵉ'ila'*, Heb. *Sha'ul*).   Modern examples are
Luser-Ludwig (Heb. *'El'azar*), Moses-Moritz, Isaak-Isidor (or
Ignaz).

IV. PARALLEL EXPRESSIONS

'Εκκλησία being a Greek word for a Biblical matter, it is not surprising that the latter does not stand or fall with the former. Thus it often happens in the N.T. that the word itself is missing where the matter itself is under discussion. Most important in this connection is I Peter, which, though Pauline in its general attitude, nevertheless differs from Paul in not using the word ἐκκλησία [1]; for this Epistle contains a specially rich analysis of the nature of the ἐκκλησία of God: "An elect race, a royal priesthood, a holy nation, a people for God's own possession" (ii, 9—all from the O.T.); "A spiritual house" (ii, 5); "The people of God" (ii, 10). Cf. Paul's strong emphasis in Phil. iii, 3: "We are the circumcision". It is the same in other passages: "Israel" (Rom. ix, 6); "the Israel of God" (Gal. vi, 16); "Israel after the spirit" (implied at I Cor. x, 18); "Abraham's seed, heirs according to the promise" (Gal. iii, 29; cf. Heb. ii, 16); "Twelve Tribes" (James i, 1). The fact of the Dispersion brings a new aspect of the matter into view, showing that Christians, just because they are the ἐκκλησία, are "sojourners of the Dispersion" (I Pet. i, 1) and "the Twelve tribes that are in the Dispersion" (James i, 1).

Other designations, only loosely connected with the O.T., or entirely apart from it, do not conflict with the proper title of ἐκκλησία. Some of them describe the faith and ideals of Christians, e.g. "the saints"

[1] Cf. Th. Spörri, Der Gemeindegedanke im ersten Petrusbrief (1925), esp. pp. 271 ff.; [E. G. Selwyn, I Peter, pp. 81-90, 153-168.]

(generally with a reference to the O.T.) ; " the faithful " ; " the brethren " ; " the brotherhood ". Others are related to special circumstances and disappear later, e.g., " the disciples " (μαθηταί) ; " the poor ". The designation of Christians as " disciples " is applied to the first followers of Jesus, then widened, then narrowed and finally relegated to the background, simply because of the special relationship between the first followers and their master. There is no ground for speaking of a development from one designation to another, culminating in ἐκκλησία.[1]

The expression συναγωγή stands in a class by itself ; it will be treated here only in its relation to ἐκκλησία. The superficial view commonly held is that the latter means the Christian Church and the former the Jewish Synagogue. But this neat distinction first came into vogue in later centuries, and continues into our time. It looks as though the Christian congregation could call itself συναγωγή (James ii, 2, and v, 14).[2] Less questionable than this is the fact that the Jewish Christians in Trans-Jordan used the word both for their Church fellowship and for their Church building.[3] Apart from this more or less isolated instance, Jewish Christians generally called themselves ἐκκλησία and not συναγωγή. The exact opposite is found in the case of a Marcionite συναγωγή.[4] When the separation of Jewish Christians from their mother-Church became more clearly marked, they probably called both their meetings and their meeting-places synagogues. It

---

[1] Against Harnack, Mission and Expansion I, 404 ff.

[2] Cf. Zahn, Matthew (1922), p. 546.

[3] Epiphanius, Haer, xxx. 18, 2 : πρεσβυτέρους γὰρ οὗτοι (i.e. the Christians of Transjordan) ἔχουσιν ἀρχισυναγώγους · συναγωγὴν δὲ καλοῦσιν τὴν ἑαυτῶν ἐκκλησίαν καὶ οὐχὶ ἐκκλησίαν.

[4] συναγωγὴ Μαρκιωνιστῶν : le Bas-Waddington, Inscr. Grecques et Letines III (1870), No. 2558, p. 852 ; cf. Harnack, op. cit., 421, 659. [See Schürer, G.V.I. (4), II, 517.]

would seem that at first all Christians, Jewish and
Gentile, used both expressions. It must also be remembered that there is evidence for the use of
συναγωγή by ancient heathen brotherhoods.[1] But in
spite of such analogies, an O.T. origin is even more
obvious for συναγωγή than for ἐκκλησία. And the
coupling of the two is of primary importance for the
discussion of the question, what Aramaic word was
used by the early Christians and by Jesus himself?
The question is—whether ἐκκλησία owes anything to a
Semitic equivalent, and, if so, how its meaning is
affected.

[1] Cf. W. Koester, Die Idee der Kirche, etc., n. 12., p. 1.

V. MATTHEW xvi, 18 AND xviii, 17

1. These two sayings raise many difficulties. Neither of them finds its place automatically among the ἐκκλησία passages already discussed. In fact, they demand a thorough-going criticism, especially on the part of those who accept their authenticity. Problems are presented not only by the Greek text, but also by the original Aramaic; and the main question is seriously complicated by the way in which subordinate questions impinge upon one another. Thus the exposition of the Greek text determines the choice of a Semitic word behind ἐκκλησία and *vice versa* the word chosen affects the exposition. Again, the answer to the question of authenticity depends on the nature of the exposition; and *vice versa* the exposition will be influenced if that question has been settled already on other grounds; both positive and negative answers have actually led to more or less convincing expositions. All this bears on the understanding of the Matthean use of the word ἐκκλησία. Furthermore, the linguistic question is bound up with judgments concerning history. This interaction must never be forgotten. Word, idea, and thing in this case are unusually complex—as if a mathematician were to combine imaginary quantities with real ones. But although the complication creates difficulties, it does not necessarily lead to the confusion and bewilderment which have appeared from time to time, as interpretation has swung to and fro, up and down.

2. A peculiar difficulty, which meets us on the threshold, consists in the fact that the two passages, Matt. xvi, 18 and xviii, 17, are not in the same key. If

neither is authentic, the former may mean the universal Church and the latter the individual congregation ; and there can be no doubt that this common—but not therefore correct—differentiation reacts upon the interpretation of both passages, supporting the view that they are unauthentic. But if they are authentic, the interpretation seems to be extremely difficult, taking the first to refer to the *qahal* and the second to the synagogue. How are we to explain the fact that ἐκκλησία is used for both ? We must examine again the relationship between *qahal* and synagogue. Is it certain that the former is the right word in xvi, 18 ?

3. The text of Matt. xviii, 17, and still more that of xvi, 18, are above suspicion. We have no Greek MSS. or ancient translations which do not contain Matt. xvi, 17-19 or at least xvi, 18 ; and it can safely be asserted to-day that no objection to the verses under discussion can be based on their occurrence or nonoccurrence in patristic writings from the time of Justin Martyr onwards.[1]

The persistence of a critical attitude to the text is due—apart from " Protestant ", and above all "Modernist ", efforts to get rid of the *locus classicus* for Papal primacy,[2]—to the strong impression made on many

---

[1] See K. L. Schmidt, Die Kirche, 283 ff. It must be specially emphasised that the latest critical attempt to discredit the text, as made by Harnack on the basis of a passage in St. Ephraem, has been rebutted by Catholic scholars. Cf. C. A. Kneller in Zeitschr. f. kath. Theol. (1920) 147 ff. ; J. Sickenberger, " Eine neue Deutung der Primatstelle (Matt. xvi, 18) " in Theol. Revue. (1920), 1 ff. ; S. Euringer in Festgabe f. A. Ehrhard (1922) 141 ff. ; J. Geiselmann in Bibl. Zeitfr. xii, 7 (1927) ; K. Pieper, Jesus und die Kirche, 37 ff. See Joachim Jeremias, Golgotha (1926) 68 ff.

[2] Cf. K. L. Schmidt, Die Kirche, 300 f., in opposition to J. Schnitzer, Hat Jesus das Papsttum gestiftet ? (1910) and F. Heiler, Der Katholizismus (1923) 25 ff., 39 ff.

by the fact that Matt. xvi, 18 forms part of a saying which is found in neither Mark nor Luke. Two deductions may be drawn from this : *either* Matt. xvi, 17-19 in an interpolation into the text of Matthew, *or* Matthew (or his authority) added them to an earlier text, perhaps going back to Jesus, which was known to Mark and Luke. The first is too crude to be taken very seriously. Words of such importance must be treated with great care. It is not usual in other cases to regard a passage as unauthentic because it has no parallels.[1]   But even the second, though more careful, has not the significance often attached to it. The question may certainly be raised whether these verses are interpolated by Matthew (or his authority). But that does not settle the question of the authenticity of the logion. We have to reckon with the possibility of an interpolation drawn from an otherwise unknown genuine tradition, whose value is to be tested quite apart from its present setting. Even if there are chronological and psychological questions which we cannot answer, owing to the nature of the Gospel tradition, a logion without a context has to be expounded as such.[2]

4. Literary criticism is in any case so uncertain that the wise student must direct his attention to matters of fact. All objections to the ἐκκλησία sayings in Matthew lead directly to the discussion of factual problems. The first clear point is, that Matt. xvi, 17-19

[1] Linton, in his survey (see Bibliography), p. 158, rightly says of critical objection to the text, " This by itself is not enough ; other material peculiar to individual Gospels is not judged in this rigorous way ".

[2] Cf. K. L. Schmidt, Der Rahmen der Geschichte Jesu (1919) 217 ff. Bultmann, Die Geschichte der synoptischen Tradition (1931), 277, dealing with Mark viii, 27-30, gives a different analysis. Against this, which appeared in the 1921 edition, cf. K. L. Schmidt, Die Kirche (1927) 282 n.1.

is thoroughly Semitic in character : its native place
must be within the early Christian community in
Palestine.[1]   But this does not prove it to be a genuine
saying of Jesus.   Further inquiries have still to be
made, in two directions : *first* as to Jesus and the Church
and *secondly* concerning the position of Peter in the
early Church.   Each of these includes two questions,
so that we have four subjects [2] to deal with : (*a*)
statistics relating to the fact that the word ἐκκλησία
only occurs twice in the Gospels ; (*b*) eschatology and
the question whether Jesus, as the preacher of the
Kingdom of God, could have founded a Church ;
(*c*) does Church History show Peter to have held the
position of authority ascribed to him in Matt. xvi, 18 ?
(*d*) from the point of view of psychology, did Peter
really make good as the " Rock " ?

(*a*) Mere statistics prove as little in the present case
as in I Peter, where the actual word ἐκκλησία does not
occur, but that for which it stands is indicated by an
abundance of other terms, mostly drawn from the
Old Testament.   Similar synonyms [3] are found in the
Gospel tradition.   Matt. xxvi, 31 and John x, 1
speak of the ποίμνη (flock), which at I Cor. ix, 7
quite clearly means the Church.   With this we may
compare ποίμνιον (little flock) Luke xii, 32 ; Acts
xx, 28 ; I Pet. v, 2 f. ; αὐλὴ τῶν προβάτων (sheep-
fold) John x, 1 ; ἀρνία μου (my lambs) John xxi, 15 ;
τὰ προβάτια μου (my sheep) John xxi, 16 f.   Note that
the sheep are " mine ", as the Church is at Matt. xvi,
18.   Just as the Good Shepherd is the same as the Lord

---

[1] Cf. Strack-Billerbeck ad loc. ; Bultmann, Die Gesch. d. syn.
Trad., 277 ; Jeremias, Golgotha, 68 ff.

[2] Well characterised by Linton, op. cit., pp. 175 ff.

[3] Cf. Linton, 176.   The problem of the Church in the fourth
Gospel is dealt with by E. Gaugler in Intern. Kirchl. Zeitschr.
(1924), pp. 97 ff., 181, and (1925), pp. 27 ff.   The latter, on p. 28,
treats specially of synonyms of ἐκκλησία.

so his flock is the same as his Church.   This group or
company is, to begin with, the college of the twelve
disciples appointed by Jesus.   He separated a small
band from the rest of the Jews, sharply opposed to the
Pharisaic scribes and ultimately to the whole impeni-
tent nation, to constitute the true ἐκκλησία or people
of God.   Thus Matt. xvi, 18 gives us more than an
item in the life of Jesus : this is an event in the history
of the Christ.   The existence of this inner circle of
disciples in the lifetime of Jesus is not rendered doubtful
by differences in the lists of names or by the lack of
individual characterisation.   The concrete personal
note was certainly missing at the time when these lists
were compiled, viz. in the period of the early Church.
Details were supplied later in the apocryphal Acts of
the Apostles, which were embroidered in the usual
style of Hellenistic romance.[1]   For the early Church,
on the other hand, it was more important that
Jesus had the Twelve with him than that something definite should be known about each of them.
This being so, there is no reason why we should
not accept the traditional picture of the historical
Jesus with his disciples.[2]   A deeper and broader
foundation is reached when the discussion is extended
so as to include the questions whether, and in what
sense, Jesus regarded himself as the Son of Man, and
whether, and in what manner, he instituted the Lord's

[1] Cf. K. L. Schmidt, " Die Stellung der Evangelien in der
allgemeinen Literaturgeschichte ", in Gunkel-Festschrift (1923),
II, 80.

[2] R. Schütz in Apostel und Jünger, 1921, says on the one hand,
following Wellhausen and Bultmann, " The historical college
of the Twelve cannot be earlier than the beginning of Paul's
Apostleship " (p. 75), but, on the other hand, is compelled to
agree that " the possibility that Jesus himself had already referred
to the symbolic meaning of the number, Twelve, cannot be ruled
out " (72).   [See Ed. Meyer, Urspr. u. Anf. (1924), I. 291-9.]

Supper. If Jesus understood his Messiah-ship in the
sense of Daniel vii, this will open up new vistas when we
are considering the nature and the importance of his
founding of the Church. For the Son of Man in
Daniel is not a mere individual : he is the represen-
tative of " the people of the saints of the Most High "
and has set himself the task of making this people of
God, the ἐκκλησία, a reality.[1] From this point of view
the so-called institution of the Lord's Supper can be
shown to be the formal founding of the Church.[2] Thus

[1] Three modern scholars seem to have drawn attention inde-
pendently to this aspect of the founding of the Church by Jesus
Christ. T. Schmidt, in Der Leib Christi (1919), has a section
entitled " Analogie von Messias und Gemeinde " (pp. 217 ff.).
A. Schlatter, Die Geschichte des Christus (1923), p. 375, says,
" The title, Christ, demanded of him that he should bring the
perfect community into being." Finally, the deepest insight is
shown by Kattenbusch in the Harnack Festgabe (1921), 143-172 :
" Christ has an independent existence, just as much as each of those
who are his, but is only himself in the σῶμα ; without this he
would not be what his name indicates " (145) ; " he must so shape
his personal life that he really is, and can claim to be, the type of a
people of the saints of the Most High ; and he must create and
build up this people among men " (160). These are followed
by Gloege, Reich Gottes und Kirche im N.T. (1929), 218, 228 :
" The saviour is only saviour as the creator of a new, redeemed
and justified people ; . . . the Χριστός can no more be Christ
without the ἐκκλησία than the ποιμήν can be shepherd without
the ποίμνιον." See also Linton, op. cit., 148 : " The Messiah
is no private person ; a community belongs to him ; to the
shepherd belongs the flock ".
[Reference may also be made to T. W. Manson, The Teaching
of Jesus (1931), 211-236 ; J. R. Coates, The Coming of the Church
(1929), 23-54 ; R. Newton Flew, Jesus and his Church (1938).]
[2] Again it is to Kattenbusch that we owe our deepest insight.
In the Harnack Festgabe (p. 171) he writes : " When he founds
the ἐκκλησία, a community in his name, through the Last
Supper, he does not forget the title he chose for himself out of
Daniel, but puts it in the foreground [Mark xiv, 21], indicating
the nature of the Son of Man by means of a reference to Isaiah

we not only become more and more certain that, so
far as facts are concerned, Matt. xvi, 18 does not stand
alone, but also realise—an important point—that this
conception of the complex of ideas (Jesus, Messiah,
Son of Man, Disciples, Community, Lord's Supper)
leads directly to the Pauline and sub-Pauline doctrine
of the ἐκκλησία, which on the one hand is " from
above " and on the other is " the Body of Christ ",
just as Christ is at the same time highly exalted and
present in the midst of the community.   The question
whether Jesus himself founded the Church is really the
question concerning his Messiah-ship.[1] Problems of
detail concerning time and place, which the Gospels
do not enable us to solve, are of secondary importance
when compared with this, which is the main problem.[2]

(b) How does all this fit in with the eschatology of
Jesus' proclamation of the Kingdom of God ?   After
what has been said, we can deal with this question more
briefly.   The eschatological presuppositions of Jesus'
self-designation as Son of Man, and of the institution
of the Lord's Supper, prove that the idea of the
Church also is eschatological.   But this does not mean
that Church and Kingdom of God are the same
thing.   They are not the same in the early Church,
which certainly regarded itself as the ἐκκλησία while
continuing the proclamation of the Kingdom.   Nor
are they the same in the preaching of Jesus, for he
promised the Kingdom of God to his Church, i.e. the

liii ".   This would perhaps be more impressive if the analysis of
the text were more convincing.   Cf. K. L. Schmidt on " Abend-
mahl im N.T." in Rel. Gesch. Geg., 2nd ed., I, 6 ff.

[1] Cf. the concise presentation of the affirmative view, against
Wellhausen, Wrede and Bultmann, by K. L. Schmidt in R.G.G.,
2nd ed., III, 149 f.

[2] That is what throws doubt on Wendland's otherwise attractive
picture of stages in Die Eschatologie des Reiches Gottes bei
Jesus (1931).

Church which he founded. The ἐκκλησία after Easter regarded itself as eschatological in this sense. Similarly the individual Christian may be called eschatological, because he is a justified sinner.[1]

---

[1] Bultmann's construction misses the points upon which we have here briefly touched, in his Gesch. syn. Trad. and also in his review of Wendland in Deutsche Literaturzeitung (1934), 2019 ff. When he says that the real problem of the ἐκκλησία is presented by the fact that it takes the place of the Kingdom of God, for the speedy coming of which Jesus had been looking, he is viewing the matter in the light of his earlier formulation of the question, i.e. from an evolutionary standpoint, which is not adequate for the understanding of the transition from Jesus to the community, whether of Peter or of Paul. If Bultmann agrees that the early Christians regarded themselves as the ἐκκλησία, and gave this word " a radically eschatological meaning ", it is incumbent upon him to answer the question how the early Christians distinguished between the Kingdom of God and the Church. Cf. the Preface to the 2nd impression of K. L. Schmidt, Die Kirche ; Linton, op. cit., 179 f.

J. Haller, in Das Papsttum I (1934), p. 4, lays it down that " a sober criticism, bearing in mind the whole of the Saviour's teaching, can never believe that Jesus spoke the words ascribed to him in Matthew. . . . This is a prediction introduced after the event had taken place." In a comment on this (p. 442) we read : " It is not yet settled whether the saying is authentic. In my judgment the verdict must be negative, unless we are to depart from the rules of criticism that prevail everywhere else. Many, it is true, still do this, e.g., Kattenbusch. . . . The same judgment must be passed on K. L. Schmidt's verbose and pretentious essay, in spite of its learning and ingenuity." As for " the rules of criticism that prevail everywhere else ", to which Haller appeals in the interests of " a sober criticism ", it is enough to point out that an entirely different verdict, in whole and in part, is given by the jurist, G. Holstein, in Die Grundlagen des ev. Kirchenrechts (1928) and by the historian, E. Caspar, in Geschichte des Papsttums (1930-33). Of the latter Haller (p. 441) merely remarks, " Our ways in general are so far apart, and our divergence in the assessment and treatment of sources is of so fundamental a nature, that I think it is right for me to avoid critical discussion, apart from a few cases. There are different ways of writing history, and every man must go his own way

(c) From the point of view of Church History, the argument against Matt. xvi, 18 is that Peter did not occupy the authoritative position in the early Church that has been ascribed to him. This objection, supported by reference to I Cor. iii, 11 ; x, 4 ; Eph. ii, 20 (see note on p. 15), [1] may be met by two considerations. On the one hand, Peter played a bigger part on the occasion of his condemnation by Paul than is admitted by Protestants in their controversy with Rome. Since there are no obvious historical or psychological reasons for his being singled out, the simplest solution of the problem is that he had been designated by Jesus himself. On the other hand, if Peter was faced with opposition in the early Church, in Johannine as well as Pauline circles (note the rivalry

('sehe jeder wie er's treibe')". This makes it unnecessary to say any more about Haller just now. Cf. K. Pieper, Die angebliche Einsetzung des Petrus? (1935) ; Jesus und die Kirche (1932).

The latest writer who deals with this subject, W. G. Kümmel, in "Die Eschatologie der Evangelien" (Theol. Blätt., 1936, 225 ff.) fails to explain the special eschatological character of the ἐκκλησία over against the Kingdom of God, and writes as follows (p. 231). "K. L. Schmidt seeks the support of linguistic research for the view that Jesus intended to found a special community, and employs Matt. xvi, 18 as evidence, regarding it as authentic. It is characteristic how in this whole discussion systematic construction takes the place of an exegetical formulation of the question. But a true Biblical theology must start from a strict exegesis." To such a "critical" pronouncement it can only be replied that the present re-statement and enlargement of our interpretation of the locus classicus ecclesiae does not start from a "systematic construction", but from "an exegetical formulation of the question", and therefore what the writer is concerned with is precisely a "true Biblical theology", consistent with a "strict exegesis". [See G. D. Kilpatrick, The Origins of the Gospel acc. to St. Matthew (1946), pp. 39 f. : " . . . these sections may well have a basis in unwritten tradition" ; G. Johnston, The Church in the N.T. (1943), 48-51, is negative.]

[1] According to H. Windisch in Theol. Rundsch. (1933), p. 251, "to-day it is only the third objection which has any real weight".

between Peter and the other disciple, John xx, 2 ff.),
it is not easy to see how Matt. xvi, 18 could have arisen
out of such a situation. The theory of a prediction
after the event comes to grief on the fact that the
" event " for Peter is very different from what might
have been expected from Matt. xvi, 18. We may therefore accept the disputed text as genuine on the principle of preferring the harder reading.[1]

(d) As for the psychological objection that Peter did
not turn out to be a rock—to admit that would mean
giving up the fundamental idea of the ἐκκλησία. The
setting apart of Peter is an enigma, and must be accepted as such. Psychological theories of all sorts may
throw a certain amount of light on the subject, but
they cannot remove the final mystery. We cannot and
dare not give an answer to the question why God made
Israel his people and his Church. Peter is specially
chosen and is disobedient, but remains chosen, for
he has become the *fundamentum ecclesiae*. Israel also is
chosen and is disobedient, but remains chosen, for
there is a remnant that returns.[2]

---

[1] In connection with the many attempts to depreciate Peter
more than is permissible, here again one must not follow Luther's
exegesis, seeing in Matt. xvi, 18 nothing more than in Matt. v, 3.
Cf. K. L. Schmidt, Die Kirche, 289 ff. Strack-Billerbeck's
effort (I, 732) to put Matt. xvi, 18 back into Hebrew is vitiated
by the desire to depreciate Peter. Bultmann finds the effort
" absurd " (Gesch. d. syn. Tr., 148), but Linton says it " deserves
attention " (op. cit. 170).

[2] Cf. W. Leonhard in Una Sancta, 1927, p. 485 : " . . . the
shaky man of rock, the confessor prone to denial, the upholder who
needs upholding—that this should be the first Christian man is
indeed one of the most startling paradoxes of the Gospel ; it is a
piece of the Passion Story, and has its reflex in every Christian
life. Peter must not be depreciated. So says K. L. Schmidt
convincingly." Otherwise Leonhard disagrees with K. L. S., who
" cannot refrain from expressing the judgment that it is just the
singling-out of the personality of Simon Peter that confounds the
claims of the Roman hierarchy " ; he calls that " a Protestant

A note may be added on the difficulty, often emphasised, that " Church " is not a suitable object after the verb " to build ".[1] The figure of building is common in Judaism and early Christianity, specially for the creation of the world.[2] It might be suggested that the word " house " lies behind the word " Church" in Matt. xvi, 18.[3]

overplus " ; but that is another matter. Karl Heim makes a good point on the other side in Das Wesen des ev. Christentums (1929), p. 36 : " It is a strange irony of world history, that just these words of Christ should be displayed in gigantic letters on the dome of the Pope's great basilica—just these words of Christ which, understood in their original sense, exclude and forbid the Papacy in every form, seeing that they are practically unique in assigning to the apostle a peerless and absolutely unrepeatable position in God's spiritual temple ".

W. G. Kümmel (op. cit.), p. 232, can only say here, " It is entirely inconceivable that Jesus should have conferred on a man the control of admission into the Kingdom of God ". To this it may be replied that, as indicated in the text above, everything becomes inconceivable if Matt. xvi, 18 is regarded as an invention of the community.

K. Pieper starts from Catholic premises in his controversy with K. L. S. and Karl Heim, in Jesus und die Kirche, pp. 60 ff. It is characteristic that according to him J. Geiselmann (see p. 36, n. 1) declares that " we must bear in mind that there are limits to what the Bible alone can tell us of what the Lord's promise involves in detail concerning the Petrine primacy " ; and that J. Sickenberger, in Bibl. Zeitfragen (1929), pp. 16 ff., dealing with the confession at Caesarea Philippi, does not make the slightest reference to the bearing of Matt. xvi, 17 ff. on Peter's successors ; while Karl Adam, in Das Wesen des Katholizismus (1934), p. 118, expresses the opinion that the reference to Peter's successors can be denied by those who confine their attention to the Biblical text, and do not link it up with the Incarnation and its object.

[1] This is the ground on which Holtzmann (N.T. übers. I, 165 f.) decides against authenticity : " If Jesus were speaking, we should expect οἰκοδομεῖν to be followed by a concrete object, such as τὴν οἰκίαν μου ".

[2] Cf. Strack-Billerbeck, I, 732 f. ; Zahn, Matt., 547 ; Schlatter, Matt., 506 f.

[3] Cf. Hermann's careful and weighty contribution in Th. Blätt.

5. The arguments so far advanced are valid if
ἐκκλησία at Matthew xvi, 18 and xviii, 17 corresponds to the Hebrew *qahal*, as it does elsewhere in the
New Testament. But it is still an open question
whether we ought to think of Hebrew or of Aramaic.
And, further, it is not settled whether we should
confine ourselves to *qahal* or its Aramaic equivalent
qᵉhala' (a loan-word from Biblical Hebrew).

If Jesus and his disciples spoke Aramaic, it does not
necessarily follow that this was the only language they
used for religious purposes.[1] We must assume that
they had a certain familiarity with Hebrew as the
language of their ancestral Church life.[2] But this does
not point conclusively to *qahal*. We need not concern
ourselves with *qᵉhillah*, the word used by Franz Delitzsch
at Matt. xvi, 18 in his Hebrew translation of the New
Testament (1880), since it occurs so rarely in the Old
Testament and Rabbinic writings. A word to be taken
more seriously is *'edhah*,[3] which in the Old Testament
differs very little from *qahal*.

Neither of these expressions is much employed by the
Rabbis. They prefer *çibbur*, which occurs once in the
Old Testament (II Kings x, 8), meaning " heap ",
and may be said to be the proper word for the community, whether national or local, in later Judaism.[4]

(1926), pp. 203 ff. Bultmann (Trad., 149) is mistaken in calling it
" quite superfluous ", for it has the distinction of recognising the
special affinity of ἐκκλησία and οἰκία in both O.T. and N.T.
Pieper (op. cit.) has no evidence for the charge that Hermann's
suggestion would reduce the meaning of ἐκκλησία to a religious
fellowship of any kind.

[1] Cf. Dalman, Jesus-Jeshua (English Trans., Levertoff, 1929).

[2] Dalman, op. cit., refers to Luke iv, 16 as showing Jesus'
familiarity with Hebrew.

[3] See O. Procksch in Deutsche Theologie (1928), p. 23, with
answer by K. L. S. on p. 26.

[4] So Strack-Billerbeck, I, 734. See Dalman, Wörterbuch, sub
voc.

Another common expression is *k^eneṣeth Yisra'el* ; only the verb (*kanaṣ*) is found in the O.T., meaning " to gather ", " to assemble ". This word is used to emphasise the personification of the believing community of Israel.[1] Actually it is impossible to establish any real differentiation between the four terms, *qahal*, *'edhah*, *çibbur*, *k^eneṣeth*, and so no conclusions can be drawn from Hebrew usage.

Assuming the existence of an Aramaic equivalent of ἐκκλησία, we might think of *q^ehala'*, which is not pure Aramaic but borrowed from Biblical Hebrew. While this occurs in the Targums, they contain no example of an Aramaic *'edhta'* for the Hebrew *'edhah*.[2] We shall therefore do well to rule out *'edhta'*. There are examples of *çibbura'* ; but the commonest expression is *k^enishta'*.[3] Special importance attaches to this word, because it is used for ἐκκλησία and for συναγωγή in Syriac versions, whose language is closely akin to the Palestinian Aramaic of Jesus.

Of the Syriac versions, the Curetonian (3rd cent.), the Peshitta (beginning of 5th cent.) and the Philoxenian (beginning of 6th cent.) use *'edhta'* for ἐκκλησία as the Christian Church, and *k^enushta'* for συναγωγή as the Jewish synagogue ; but the Sinaitic (3rd cent., earlier than the Curetonian) uses *k^enushta'* for both. (The Sinaitic omits Matt. xvi, 18 but retains xviii, 17.) Connected with the Sinaitic is the Palestinian-Syriac version, chiefly known to us through the lectionary called *Evangeliarium Hierosolymitanum*.[4]   No precise date

---

[1] Cf. Str.-Bill, I, 734 ; Schürer, G. J. V., II, 504 : " When considered as a religious community, it is called *k^eneṣeth* ".

[2] Dalman, however, gives it as an Aramaic word.   It is not in Levy.   Wellhausen, Matt., p. 84, says it is not Palestinian but Syriac.

[3] Cf. Levy s.v.   Dalman also gives the form *k^enisṭa'* (cf. *k^eneṣeth*), as meaning synagogue, viz., the building.

[4] Edited by Lagarde in Bibl. Syr. (1892).   See Schwally,

can be assigned to this, but it certainly creates the impression that it is older than the others. The dialect in which it is written differs considerably from ordinary Syriac, and may bear a relatively close resemblance to the language of Jesus and his disciples.[1] It actually uses the Aramaic word $k^e nushta$' ($= k^e nishta$') for both the Christian ἐκκλησία and the Jewish συναγωγή.[2]

After what has been said, it seems highly probable that Jesus used the word $k^e nishta$'.[3] Now if the application of the word qahal (Aram. $q^e hala$') to the Christian Church implies its claim to be the true Church of the Old Testament, it is also possible that $k^e nishta$' is meant to indicate the whole body of that Church. At the same time we must remember that this Aramaic word, like its usual Greek equivalent, συναγωγή, means a fellowship in the narrower sense, as defined by reference to locality, membership or constitution. This points to the idea of a separatist $k^e nishta$'. Are we then to think of the early Christian Church as a sect within Judaism? Actually it was often treated as such by the Jewish authorities. Its own conviction was that it was the only synagogue entitled to claim

Idioticon des christlich-palästinischen Aram. (1893), and Schulthess, Lexicon Syro-palaestinum (1903). For all other Syr. cf. O. Klein Syrisch-griech. Wörterbuch zu den vier kanonischen Ev. (1916).

[1] So E. Nestle, Einführung in das Gr. N.T. (1909), 115 ; Schulthess, Gramm. des christlich-palästinischen Aram. (herausgeg. E. Littmann) 1924, p. 3.

[2] Cf. Schürer, II, 504 : " in Christian Palestinian Aramaic $k^e nishta$', corresponding to the Greek συναγωγή, seems to have been the usual word for Church ". Wellhausen, Matt., p. 84 : " The original Aramaic word $k^e nishta$' stands for both the Jewish and the Christian fellowship. The Palestinian Christians continued its use for both Church and Synagogue."

[3] Cf. Zahn, Matt., 546, and Merx, " Die vier kanonischen Ev. nach der syrischen im Sinai-kloster gefundenen Palimps.", Matt. (1902), 268. Joach. Jeremias, in Golgotha, p. 69, pleads for " probably çibbura'—otherwise $k^e nishta$' ".

that it embodied true Judaism, the true Israel. This was not the first time such a thing had happened. The evidence is not plentiful, but it is enough to prove the point. Reference may be made to I Maccabees ii, 42 (συναγωγὴ Ἀσιδαίων) and vii, 12 (συναγωγὴ γραμματέων) ; these might have made the same claim, though separating themselves for more scholastic reasons.[1] Here belongs also the Jewish community of " The New Covenant at Damascus ", known through the document found in the Genizah (lumber-room) of the Cairo synagogue : its members called themselves 'edhah (vii, 20 ; x, 4, 8 ; xiii, 13) or qahal (vii, 17 ; xi, 22), and felt themselves to be the " Remnant ".[2] The idea of the qᵉhal Yahwe was not only not given up ; it acquired a special significance, for such a group constituted the " Remnant ", on which Israel's standing as the people of God depended. Thus the Church of God was embodied in the synagogue of Jesus the Messiah. In this seeming paradox of a part representing the whole lies the secret of the

[1] That such a synagogue should have claimed to represent the qᵉhal Yahwe Bultmann considers " scarcely credible ". His objections, involving as they do an exaggeration of the teaching function of the synagogue, are not convincing.

[2] The text is given by Schechter in Documents of Jewish Sectaries (1910), to which our figures refer. L. Rost, in Die Damaskus-schrift (Kleine Texte 167 (1933), gives Schechter's arrangement along with another, and amends the text, reviewing all the work done on the subject up to 1933. Attempts to assign a date differ by centuries. Bertholet, in Rel. Gesch. Geg., 2nd ed., I, 1775 f. (Damaskusschrift), suggests the Maccabean or the Roman period, perhaps 1st century B.C. G. Hölscher, Gesch. der isr. u. jüd. Rel. (1922), and others (see Rost, p. 4) think the documents come from precursors of the Karaites referred to by Kirkisani (10th cent.) as " sons of Zadok ".
[See Foakes Jackson and Kirsopp Lake, The Beginnings of Christianity, Vol. I, pp. 97-101 ; R. H. Charles, Between the Old and New Testaments, pp. 234-236, and Apocr. and Pseudepigr., II, 785 ff.]

genuine synagogue and of the genuine congregation of Jesus Christ. The famous founding of the ἐκκλησία by Jesus simply means this combined separation and concentration of his band of disciples (Matt. xvi, 18). All that we know of the attitude of Jesus towards the q^{e}hal Yahwe gains breadth and depth, and colour too, when we recognise his concern with the k^{e}nishta'.[1]

Finally this view makes the connection clear between Matt. xvi, 18 and Matt. xviii, 17. In the latter passage, the command to report an erring brother's fault to the ἐκκλησία should not be explained as obviously an item from an early Christian catechism,[2] but understood as referring to the synagogue, the Old Testament congregation. Jesus' attitude to that institution is not negative but positive. Indeed it is he, and only he, who brings it to perfection, taking his stand as Messiah, here as elsewhere, under the Law.[3]

---

[1] Bultmann (Trad. 149 f.) shows a complete misunderstanding when he asserts that it makes no difference for Matt. xvi, 18 f. whether ἐκκλησία represents qahal or 'edhah or k^{e}nishta'.

[2] Evidence for this common " critical " view need not be given.

[3] Cf. K. L. Schmidt, " Die Verkündigung des N.T. in ihrer Einheit und Besonderheit " (Th. Blätt. (1931), Sp. 120) ; " Das Christuszeugnis der synoptischen Ev." (Kirchenbl. f. d. ref. Schweiz (1933), 403), which also appears as " Jesus Christus im Zeugnis der Heiligen Schrift und der Kirche " (Sammelband (1936), 22). [See G. Johnston, The Church in the N.T., 140.]

VI. OLD TESTAMENT AND JUDAISM

1. *Greek Judaism.* (*a*) The word ἐκκλησία occurs about 100 times in the LXX, and occasionally in Aquila, Symmachus and Theodotion. The Hebrew equivalent is almost always *qahal*. The only exceptions to be noted in the LXX are as follows : I Sam. xix, 20 (*lahᵃqah*) ; Neh. v, 7 (*qᵉhillah*) ; Ps. xxv (Heb. xxvi), 12 (*maqhelim*) ; Ps. lxvii (Heb. lxviii), 27 (*maqheloth*). The usage is thus uniform and clear. The Hebrew words just mentioned all come from the root *qahal*. In the case of *lahᵃqah* the radical letters are found in a different order : this may point to some derivative of *qahal*, or may be due to dittography, coming so soon after *laqahath*.[1]

In the LXX ἐκκλησία has no ecclesiastical significance ; it simply means " gathering ", and denotes either coming together, as at Deut. ix, 10 ; xviii, 16 (*yom haqqahal* : Luther " Versammlung " ; R.V. " assembly ") or being together, as at I Kings viii, 65 (*qahal gadhol* : Luther " Versammlung " ; R.V. " congregation "). The nature of the gathering depends entirely upon the nature of those who compose it. Thus at I Sam. xix, 20 we have " the company (ἐκκλησίαν) of the prophets ", and at Ecclus. xxvi, 5 the context justifies " a concourse of the rabble " [Oesterley] as the translation of ἐκκλησίαν ὄχλου.[2] The

---

[1] So Gesenius-Buhl s. v.

[2] V. Ryssel, in Kautzsch's Apokr. und Pseudepigr., renders " Zusammenrottung des Pöbels ", arguing for *qᵉhalah* as the Hebr. original, against Fritzsche, who suggests *qᵉlalah* and regards LXX as a mistranslation. But perhaps Fritzsche is right, since elsewhere in Ecclus. ἐκκλησία is always a technical term for the congregation of Israel.

meaning, " People of God ", is first indicated by the
addition to ἐκκλησία of the word κυρίου (Lord, i.e.
Yahwe) : Deut. xxiii, 2 ff; I Chron. xxviii, 8 ; Neh.
xiii, 1 ; Micah ii, 5 ; cf. ἐκκλησίαν σου (*qahal lakh*,
" thy congregation ") at Lam. i, 10 ; ἐ. τοῦ ὑψίστου
at Ecclus. xxiv, 2 ; τοῦ λαοῦ τοῦ θεοῦ at Judges xx, 2.
The word " Israel " is often added : I Kings viii, 14, 22,
55 ; I Chron. xiii, 2 ; II Chron. vi, 3, 12 f. ; Ecclus.
l, 13 ; I Macc. iv, 59.   Less frequent are the attributes
" of the children of Israel " (Ecclus, l, 20) ; " of
Judah " (II Chron. xx, 5, xxx, 25) ; " of the holy
ones " (Ps. lxxxviii, 6 [R.V. lxxxix, 5]) ; " of the
saints " (Ps. cxlix, 1) ; " in Jerusalem " (I Macc. xiv,
19) ; " of the captivity " [Ezra x, 8].   There are
also passages in which ἐκκλησία, standing by itself,
means the congregation of God.   The context often
makes this quite clear.   Examples are so numerous,
especially in Chronicles, Psalms and certain Apocryphal
books, that the word must be regarded as a technical
term.   Now and then, of course, the matter is doubtful.
In any case, such additional words as " of God "
must be either expressed or understood.   The importance of the community in its gathered form is shown
by the frequency with which it is described as " the
whole community ".   The plural occurs at Ps. xxv, 12
(R.V. xxvi, 12) ; lxvii, 27 (R.V. lxviii, 26) ; the MSS.
of Ps. cvi (cvii), 32 vary between singular and plural.
The coupling of ἐκκλησία and συναγωγή at Prov. v,
14 shows how far the former is from having an established technical sense.   The translator is puzzled to
know how to render two expressions which obviously
mean the same thing: [thus A.V. and R.V. have
" congregation and assembly ", J. Moffatt " community ", A. R. Gordon " assembled community "].

The verb ἐκκλησιάζω (ἐξεκκλησιάζω) occurs at Lev.
viii, 3 ; Numb. xx, 8 ; Deut. iv, 10, xxxi, 12, 28 ;

I Kings viii, 1, xii, 21 ; I Chron. xiii, 5, xv, 3, xxviii, 1 ;
II Chron. v, 2 and elsewhere for the Hiph'il of *qahal*,
which is also rendered by συναθροίζω (Exod. xxxv,
1), συνάγω (Numb. i, 18, viii, 9, x, 7), and ἐπισυνίστημι
(Numb. xvi, 19)—all meaning " assemble " (transi-
tive). Ἐξεκκλησιάζομαι occurs at Josh. xviii, 1 ;
Judges xx, 1 ; II Sam. xx, 14 and elsewhere, meaning
" assemble " (reflexive), and representing the Niph'al
of *qahal*, which is also rendered by συνίσταμαι (Aq.,
Theod., ἐκκλησιάζομαι), Exod. xxxii, 1, and συναθροί-
ζομαι Josh. xxii, 12.

The situation is the same with regard to the more or
less technical use of the word συναγωγή. It is often
defined by a following Genitive : " company of
peoples ", Gen. xxviii, 3, xlviii, 4 ; " company of
nations ", Gen. xxxv, 11 ; " assembly of evil-doers ",
Ps. xxii, 16 (LXX xxi, 17) ; " multitude of the bulls ",
Ps. lxviii, 30 (LXX lxvii, 31) ; " congregation of
violent men ", Ps. lxxxvi, 14 (LXX lxxxv, 14) ; cf.
Jer. xliv, 15 (LXX li, 15), l, 9 (LXX xxvii, 9). On
the other hand, like ἐκκλησία, it is sometimes followed
by " of the Lord ", corresponding to *qᵉhal Yahwe* or
'adath Yahwe : Numb. xx, 4, xxvii, 17, xxxi, 16 ;
cf. Ps. lxxiv, 2 (LXX lxxiii, 2).

The result of this comparative study of ἐκκλησία
and συναγωγή is that (1) both words have more or
less the same meaning and often represent the Hebrew
word *qahal* ; (2) both have sometimes a technical and
sometimes a general meaning, as is shown in the
differing translations, " assembly ", " congregation ",
" company ", etc.

(b) The situation is the same in Philo and Josephus,
though they make more use of the words in the
technical sense which they have in secular Greek ;
the reference is often to public meetings for political
or other purposes.

5

Philo combines ἐκκλησίαι with ἀγοραί (Spec. Leg. II,
44) and with βουλαί (Omn. Prob. Lib. 138) ; cf. also
Abr. 20. He speaks of the ἐκκλησία " of God " or
" of the Lord " in connection with Deut. xxiii (Leg.
All. III, 8, 81 ; Ebr. 213) ; cf. Poster. C. 143. At
Mut. Nom. 204 he puts " of the Ruler of all "
for " of God ". His Hellenism shows itself very
clearly in his addition of the word θεία (divine)
to ἐκκλησία (Conf. Ling. 144) ; cf. Leg. All. III, 81.
Nowhere in LXX or N.T. is the Church spoken of as
divine, or as sacred (ἱερά)—though Philo uses the
latter epithet at Somn. II, 184, 187 ; Deus Imm. 111 ;
Migr. Abr. 69 ; cf. Aet. Mund. 13.[1]

Josephus, who likes to avoid ἅγιος, using θεῖος or
ἱερός instead, might well have spoken of the ἐκκλησία
as Philo did ; but he only applies it to secular gatherings, dissociating it from religion, as he does in the case
of βασιλεία [2] : see Ant. xix, 332, xvi, 62, xvii, 161,
xiv, 150 ; Vit. 37 ; Bell. iv, 255, vii, 412.

2. *Hebrew Text.* The term *qahal* and words of
similar meaning, such as *'edhah*, have already received
adequate treatment, with a view to explaining their
Greek equivalents. It remains to reverse the process,
and use the Greek words to explain the Hebrew.
While *qahal* usually becomes ἐκκλησία, this is not
always the case. It is so in Joshua, Judges, Samuel
(except I Sam. xix, 20), Kings, Chronicles, Ezra,
Nehemiah, and in Deuteronomy (except v, 22) ;
in the rest of the Pentateuch *qahal* is translated
συναγωγή, which elsewhere represents *'edhah*. (G.
Bertram points out that Origen's parallel texts sometimes have ἐκκλησία for the LXX συναγωγή : Ἄλλος at
Lev. iv, 14, 21 ; Jer. xxxiii, 17 ; Aquila at Jer. li, 15 ;
Ezek. xxvi, 7 ; Theodotion at Ezek. xxvi, 7 ; xxvii, 27 ;

[1] Cf. θεῖος and ἱερός in Cremer-Kögel.
[2] Cf. Schlatter, Matt., 508 ; Theol. des Judentums, 90 f.

xxxii, 22.) *'edhah* occurs more frequently than *qahal*
in Exod., Lev., Numb., and is almost always translated
συναγωγή—never ἐκκλησία. Joshua and Judges have
'edhah more often than *qahal*, but subsequent books
show an increasing preference for the latter. The
Psalter always uses ἐκκλησία for *qahal*, except at Ps. xl,
10 (xxxix, 11), where Aq. and Theod. have ἐκκλησία,
but LXX συναγωγή. The absence of a consistent
usage in translation shows that neither of these
Hebrew words is in itself a technical term. It only
becomes one when it is coupled with Yahwe or with
Israel as the people of Yahwe, whether in the text or
to be understood. This is shown even more clearly
by those cases in which other Greek words are used for
qahal : ὄχλος at Jer. xxxi, 8 (LXX xxxviii, 8) ; Ezek.
xvi, 40 ; xxiii, 46 f. (Aq. and Theod. ἐκκλησία) ;
πλῆθος at Exod. xii, 6 ; II Chron. xxxi, 18 ; σύστασις
at Gen. xlix, 6 ; συνέδριον at Prov. xxvi, 26.[1]

[1] M. Noth expresses a different view in Das System der zwölf
Stämme Israels (1930), 102 f., n. 2 : " We need not hesitate to derive
the words *'edhah* and *qahal* from the terminology of the amphictyony of ancient Israel ; and it is not surprising that words bound
up with a sacral institution—apart from the few places in the O.T.
which come directly from the amphictyony tradition itself—
should first reappear in the Priestly writings. . . . *Qahal*
obviously indicates the gathering, and *'edhah* the people united in
such a gathering. The latter is called *'am ha'elohim* at Judges xx, 2,
because the bond of union was the same Covenant-God and his
cult."

After the present essay was finished, L. Rost, who saw the
proofs, put the following statement at my disposal. " It is
usual to find the roots of the ἐκκλησία in the O.T. *'edhah* and
qahal. Of course the former belongs to the early history of the
synagogue, and here we are only concerned with the latter.
Qahal (a noun related to *qol* [voice], of which verbal forms,
causative and reflexive, are in frequent use) means in the oldest
passages the ' call-up ' of the people, viz., its men, for counsel or
war. It is so in Genesis xlix, 6 and Numbers xxii, 4. It looks as
if *qahal* means the community at Numbers xvi, 33, with a meaning

on which light is thrown by Micah ii, 5. The prophet speaks there of the *qᵉhal Yahwe*, the united people (Volksgesamtheit) of Yahwe, the call to unity coming from Yahwe. Deut. (xxiii, 2 ff.), uses the same phrase in the same way when it lays down conditions for the admission of the maimed or of foreigners. Deut. also justifies the coupling together of the two words ; see v, 22 (Heb. 19) ; ix, 10 ; x, 4 ; xviii, 16. The *qahal* which first established the connection between Yahwe and his people is the Sinai gathering ; the day on which this great event took place is ' the day of the *qahal* '. This is why the word *qahal* is used for the worshipping community when Solomon dedicates the Temple (I Kings viii, 14 ff.), and later for the gathering at the Feast of Tabernacles in the year 444,¹ when Ezra read the Law in the presence of men, women and children. While the *qahal* makes its appearance on special occasions of cultic importance, the old secular usage continues alongside ; *qahal* is still the call-up of a people for war ; e.g. I Sam. xvii, 47 and Ezek. xxiii, 24, 46, etc. A call-up of a different kind is the summoning of an extraordinary gathering of the people, such as Jer. xxvi, 17 and xliv, 15 mention—the former of men only, the second including women and children. To sum up, *qahal* may be defined as a gathering summoned in extraordinary circumstances, whether of men only, as in the case of war, or of a suddenly convened judicial assembly, or of the whole people, as specially in the case of Ezra. As signifying a meeting constituted by means of a call-up, the term thus comes to indicate those who are qualified to take part, as in Deut. xxiii. The development of the idea in the direction of the N.T. *ἐκκλησία* is bound up with the fact that the word was used for those who shared in the covenant at Sinai, and also for those who renewed their devotion to the Law under Ezra. Thus *qahal* is seen to connote those to whom belong the covenant and the promises. A second important point is that at least from the time of Ezra (cf. also Jer. xliv, 15) women and children were included. Thus, in its LXX form *ἐκκλησία* it commends itself to Christians, whose community welcomes women and children, in preference to *συναγωγή* whose responsibilities were confined to men. (See my forthcoming book, Die A.T. Vorstufen von Kirche und Synagoge.)" [On *ἐκκλησία* in LXX cf. J. Y. Campbell in J.T.S., 1948, pp. 130–142.]

¹ [Or 397.]

VII. ETYMOLOGY?

WE have left the etymology of the word ἐκκλησία to the end, because its history is more important. If the N.T. ἐκκλησία, coming by way of the LXX, is the fulfilment of the O.T. *qahal*, and if we associate it with *kᵉnishta'* as representing *qahal*, then there is nothing to be gained by stressing the derivation of the noun ἐκκλησία from the verb ἐκκαλεῖν and connecting it with the adjective ἔκκλητος. It is obviously significant that neither of these two words occurs in the N.T. The LXX only uses the verb at Gen. xix, 5 and Deut. xx, 10 (Heb. *qara'*), and the adjective at Ecclus. xlii, 11. Both are fairly common in classical Greek, ἔκκλητος being a technical term in connection with the ἐκκλησία as the political assembly ; cf. Xenophon, Hist. Gr., II, iv, 38, where the ἔκκλητοι are the members of the national council which takes the place of the ἐκκλησία in aristocratic states like Sparta ; cf. also Euripides, Orestes, 612, 949.

We do not know whether Paul and others were thinking of the doctrine of election when they used the word ἐκκλησία ; it is possible, but unlikely. If it were so, one might have expected to find it in passages like Eph. v, 25 ff ; I Tim. iii, 15 ; Heb. xii, 23.[1] The

---

[1] A. Jehle rightly calls attention to this passage, in his short article " *ΕΚΚΛΗΣΙΑ*, a humble request to the exegetes " (Württemberg ev. Kirchenblatt (1934), p. 78), and stresses, on the whole rightly, the questionableness—if not the irrelevance—of the etymology of ἐκκλησία. But when he says he has written " in the hope of getting the final answer through Prof. Kittel's work " (meaning the present essay), it must be laid down that the answer has already been given in the recent publications of Kattenbusch, K. L. Schmidt and others.

It is significant that those Christians who still speak Greek obviously have no need to explain etymologically how their

truth in matters of verbal usage is not to be reached by adventurous ingenuity, but by a careful study of the actual use and abuse of words. There are theologians who like to connect " Sünde " (sin) with " Sonderung " (being sundered, i.e., from God), which looks quite reasonable in German. There are philosophers who interpret " Zufall " (chance) literally as " Zu-fall " (that which befalls in an existential sense), which also looks quite artistic in German. But all that is pseudo-philology, even though it may be associated with true ideas, as in the case of Paul's queer allegorising. Ἐκκλησία is in fact that group of human beings which is called out of the world by God, even without any conscious emphasis on the preposition, like the original q͑hal Yahwe, in which no preposition is expressed.

The importance of the history of a word, with its

own word *ekklesia* has come to have its historic meaning. P. Bratsiotis, of Athens, has sent the following communication to the present writer, by request : " Ἐκκλησία in modern Greek, though properly denoting a place of worship (ναός), also has all the meanings of your word, ' Church '. For your word ' congregation ' we say either ἐκκλησία or ἐνορία, though the latter properly means ' parish '. [I. Kykkotis' Modern Greek Dictionary (1942) gives ἐκκλησίασμα for " congregation ".] There is no work on ἐκκλησία in modern Greek, except what is to be found in theological hand-books, in which there is no special philological treatment of the subject." Just as Israelites and Greek Christians appropriated a political terminology long ago, so to-day new converts outside Christendom find suitable expressions for their standing as Christians in their own language and culture. An illustration may be taken from a letter of the missionary, E. Peyer, of St. Gall : " Among the Duala people [West Africa] Christians are called *bona-Kristo*—clansmen of Christ. The word *bona* means family, kin, clan. For the word ' congregation ', *mwemba* has been chosen. This means originally an age-group, e.g., of those born in the same year or half-year, who have certain common rites to perform in youth, and specially in adolescence. The term thus indicates a clearly defined group, with restricted admission."

use and abuse, is shown by the fact that, if we were
aiming at an exact reproduction of Biblical usage in
the case of ἐκκλησία we ought always to say " assembly (of God) ".   But we cannot do so, because language
is not amenable to a dictatorial standard, and in
the present instance, owing to the wide reach of the
expression, we need both the word " Church " and
the word " congregation ".   There is something to be
said both for and against both of these.   The former indicates the one great world-wide Christian community
but on the other hand may suggest the Catholic
hierarchy ;   the latter draws attention to the small
fellowship which is also Church, but may seem to
imply Congregationalism or sectarianism.   Having
regard to its etymology, we should prefer to say
" Church " which is derived from κύριος and means
" belonging to the Lord ".   But the word has so many
meanings that it will not do by itself.   Perhaps the
" Assembly of God " might be called the " Church
community ".[1]

[1] Luther's aversion to the word " Kirche " is well-known.   It
is less widely-known that the word does not occur in the revised
text of Luther's Bible, or in a corresponding concordance,
but was actually used by Luther, mostly to denote heathen shrines
in the O.T., while it is only found at John x, 22 in the N.T., in the
compound " Church-dedication ".   Cf. W. Rotscheidt's attractive presentation of this subject in Deutsches Pfarrerblatt (1930),
pp. 506 f.
    The derivation from κύριος is not absolutely certain.   Cf.
R. Hildebrand in Deutsches Wörterbuch V, 790 s.v. : " the source
is much disputed ; in any case it is foreign, introduced along
with Christianity.   J. Grimm (Gramm. 3, 156), like Lipsius and
others, favoured derivation from the Latin circus, in early forms
such as chirih, chirch, etc. ; evidence for this was found in the gloss
in Kero [8th cent. Benedictine]—uzzana chirih, foris oratorio—
but this was corrected by Hattemer (Denkmale des Mittel-
alters (1844), p. 94) to uzzana chirihhun."   This reference to
circus, which is unanimously repudiated by German philologists,
may have something to do with the fact that Karl Barth writes in

Credo (1935) : " Ecclesia is a gathering brought together by
means of a call-up. The Germanic equivalent, *Kirche, Kerk,
Church,* is not, in my opinion, as is commonly said, a mutilated
form of the Greek adjective κυριακή (ἐκκλησία), but points back
to the root seen, e.g., in the Latin words, *circa, circum, circare,
circulus,* etc. Thus it signifies a particular room or space marked
off and to that extent given prominence." How completely
unessential etymology is for the understanding of the thing itself
may be shown by the fact that the word for Church in the
language of the Engadine and S. Tyrol is *baselgia,* in Rumanian
biserica, in Albanian *bijeske*—all from *basilica,* making their
contribution to the history of building ; (see W. Meyer-Lübke,
Roman. Etymolog. Wörteb. (1935), s.v. basilica ; J. Jud, Zur
Geschichte der bündner-roman. Kirchenspr. (1919), passim) ; the
thing itself is there without the etymology ! Finally, Luther's
Larger Catechism contains an etymological curiosity (II, 3 : see
J. T. Müller, Die symb. Bücher der ev.-luth. Kirche (1860),
p. 457) : " The little word, Church, then, means nothing else but
a general gathering, and is really not German but Greek, like
ecclesia, the original word being *Kyria,* which becomes *curia* in
Latin." Luther turns Tertullian's interpretation into etymology.
After consulting the relevant modern German dictionaries
(Weigand, neu bearb. Hirt, 1909 ; Kluge, bearb. Götze, 1934 ;
Paul, herausg. Euling, 1935) and on the advice of W. Altwegg
(Basel) and A. Debrunner (Bern), I applied to A. Götze, of Giessen,
as the greatest authority on the subject, and he has sent me the
following communication : " We German philologists are beginning to understand the word ' Kirche ' a little better. We have
abandoned both Luther's derivation from the Latin *curia*—
obviously a bright idea suggested by his visit to Rome—and
Grimm's suggestion of the Latin *circus.* It is now clear that it must
come from κυρικόν which is the common form, current in the 4th
century, of the older κυριακόν, and means a place of worship
(Gotteshaus). Words taken over from Latin in the ecclesiastical
sphere, like ' Papst ' and ' Propst,' have the final consonants un-
shifted, which means that they were not current in Germany about
600 A.D. (' Kelch ' came in with vine-growing ; ' Kreuz ' has its
' z ', not through shifting, but from the Latin *crucem,* retaining the
' ts ' sound of the second ' c '.) ' Kirche ', on the other hand, has
the ordinary German ch for k (Swiss-German still keeps the second
ch), was therefore already here before 600, and accordingly must
have been brought by an earlier wave of missionary activity than
that which gave us words like ' Papst ', etc. Which wave it was,

is under dispute.   Kluge pointed to the Gothic *kyriko*, connecting
it with an early Gothic-Arian wave, which must have reached
S.E. Germany while Theodoric the Great's kingdom was con-
tiguous with the duchy of Bavaria—and he died in 526.   I retained this in the 11th edition of Kluge, in which the ' Kirche '
article was completed in 1934 ; his reasons are fully given in
' Gotische Lehnworte im Althochdeutschen ' (Beitr. z. Gesch.
der deutschen Spr. u. Lit. (1909), pp. 124 ff.), which is still worth
reading.   Modern philologists are agreed that Arian missionaries
carried a number of ecclesiastical words up the Danube and down
the Rhine ; the question whether ' Kirche ' was one of them has
been raised by Th. Fring in Teuthonista (1932), 24, 31, 37 f., 46, 50,
120.   He supposes that κυρικόν, assuming a Feminine form
under the influence of *basilica*, arrived by way of Marseilles,
Lyon and Trèves, and puts ' Kirche ' into a group of Rhineland
Christian words, for which he gives good grounds, but I am still
in the dark as to where ' Kirche ' comes in, as no evidence is given
for it.   It is quite true that there is no literary evidence for the
Gothic *kyriko*, since Ulfilas died before it arrived, but the Old
Slavonic *cruky* and the Russian *cerkovi* may serve as witnesses.
So the question of route is still unsettled ; W. Betz, who is re-
sponsible for the word ' Kirche ' in the Trübner Deutsch. Wörterb.,
which I am now editing, will have to make up his mind about it."

VIII. APOSTOLIC FATHERS AND EARLY CATHOLICISM

THE idea of the ἐκκλησία underwent a shifting of emphasis among the Apostolic Fathers and in early Catholicism, even before the N.T. was completed.[1] Titular definition by means of adjectives became frequent though this is not found in the N.T. Whereas in the latter we only touch the fringe of speculation concerning the nature of the Church, this was now the general rule, finding expression in the use of a variety of predicates.

The oldest Christian literature, outside the N.T., makes comparatively little use of the term ἐκκλησία. The one exception is The Shepherd of Hermas. Here it denotes an individual, of whom the author becomes aware in his visions—the "Lady" (κυρία) who belongs to the "Lord" (κύριος) and is dignified with the epithet ἁγία (holy): Vis. I. i, 6;[2] I. iii, 4; IV. i, 3. The "Lady", characterised as πρεσβυτέρα (aged) because of her appearance, is described as the form (μορφή) of a "Holy Spirit", who again is identical with the "Son of God". The Pauline and sub-Pauline thought of the Church as the one body is pictured in the Parables as "a tower made as it were of one stone" (Sim. IX. xviii, 3).

The First Epistle of Clement only mentions the ἐκκλησία in three passages all reminiscent of the N.T. :

[1] The fullest statistics and information are in Kattenbusch, Harnack Festgabe (1921), 146 ff., developing his thesis in Das apostolische Symbol II (1900), 683 ff.

[2] The idea that the world was created for the sake of the Church corresponds to the Jewish idea that Israel is the goal of creation ; see Dibelius, Der Hirt des Hermas (1923) ad loc.

in the introduction, " the church of God sojourning at Rome " greets " the Church of God sojourning at Corinth " ; at xliv, 3, reference is made to " the consent of the whole Church ", and at xlvii, 6, to the " ancient Church of the Corinthians ".

Ignatius not only addresses the Churches as being in certain places, Ephesus, etc., but also gives them impressive epithets : " worthy of all felicitation " (Eph.) ; " blessed through the grace of God " (Magn.); " holy, elect and worthy of God " (Trall.) ; " which hath found mercy in the bountifulness (μεγαλειότητι) of the Father " (Rom.—with about a dozen other predicates) ; " which has found mercy and is firmly established " (Phil.) ; " filled with faith and love " (Smyrn.). The language is really excessive. Much of it is dogmatic in character, and of general application, while much is only relevant to the particular situation. One remarkable passage (Eph. v) speaks of believers as being closely joined with the bishop " as the Church is with Jesus Christ and as Jesus Christ is with the Father, that all things may be harmonious in unity ". God, Christ, and the Church form a single entity, as in the N.T. The rise of the monarchical bishop must be understood in this connection. The predicate " catholic " makes its first appearance at Smyrn. viii, where it may mean simply " one and only " (una sancta), though later it came to mean " universal ".[1] It is worth noting that the Roman Church has adopted both the Greek words ἐκκλησία and καθολική.

Polycarp greets the Philippians as a " sojourning Church " (ἐκκλησία παροικοῦσα), like Clement address- ing the Corinthians, and similarly, in Mart. Pol., the Smyrnaean Christians say, " The Church of God sojourning (παροικοῦσα) at Smyrna to the Church of God sojourning (παροικούσῃ) in Philomelium and to

[1] So Kattenbusch, op. cit., 148. [See J. B. Lightfoot, ad loc.]

all the sojourning communities of the holy and catholic Church (πάσαις ταῖς . . . τῆς ἁγίας καὶ καθολικῆς ἐκκλησίας παροικίαις) everywhere." [LXX πάροικος is for Heb. *ger*, " resident alien ". Hence comes Eng. " parish ", through Lat. *paroecia*.]   Each of these local congregations regards itself as something unique and holy, and ascribes the same dignity to its sister-congregations.   On the one hand the Church belongs to the world in which it lives, without being of it, and on the other hand it belongs to God.[1]

Four passages in the Didache mention the ἐκκλησία : iv, 14 is reminiscent of Matt. xviii, 17 ; ix, 4 and x, 5 correspond to what the N.T. says about the relation of the Church to the Kingdom ; the difficult phrase μυστήριον κοσμικὸν ἐκκλησίας, xi, 11, recalls Colossians and Ephesians, but seems to go beyond them in the direction of esoteric knowledge on the part of believers.

The so-called " Second Epistle of Clement " develops this last tendency still further when it describes the Church as " the first, the spiritual, which was created before the sun and the moon ", and goes on to adduce verses of Scripture in support of its doctrine.

The idea of the pre-existence of the Church, according to which it comes before the Synagogue, was based on Pauline (Rom. iv, 9 ff.) and sub-Pauline (Eph. i, 3 ff.) teaching, and was developed among the Valentinian Gnostics into speculation concerning Ἐκκλησία as one of the Aeons [constituting the divine *Pleroma*].   Similarly the doctrine that the Church is from above (ἄνωθεν) became a far-reaching

---

[1] Barnabas shows that, as in the N.T., the word ἐκκλησία does not settle everything, for he never speaks of Christians as ἐκκλησία but frequently refers to them as λαός, i.e., the people entrusted by God to his beloved Son (v, 7 ; vii, 5).   Elsewhere he speaks of the Temple of God (iv, 11), or the City (xvi, 5).

[On πάροικοι see E. G. Selwyn on I Pet. ii, 11.]

speculation, which afforded consolation to the representatives of a "theologia gloriae" when they were concerned about the contrast between the empirical Church and the ideal.[1] So there arose the conception of the twofold nature of the Church, as militant and triumphant. These speculations were the cause of a surprising lack of clarity in what was said about the Church, among the Greek and Latin Church Fathers. Augustine, the greatest of them, whose comprehensive mind was responsible for putting the Church at the centre of Roman Catholic thinking, is precisely the one who fails to make clear the distinction between the empirical Church and the ideal. Gnosticism having largely failed, Platonism held the field in matters of speculation, though it also left room for widely differing views, determined by the amount of emphasis given to the gulf between reality and idea. Protestantism is also under the influence of this unrealistic Platonism when it differentiates between the Church visible and the Church invisible.

[1] As Kattenbusch well puts it (op. cit., 155), " It is true that, after a certain time, the idea that the community comes ἄνωθεν became speculative ; it was not so at first."

IX. CONCLUSIONS

WHERE, when, and how does Catholicism begin, as distinct from early Christianity? The switch-over is not nearly so easy to understand as the original meaning of ἐκκλησία. The early Christian writings outside the N.T. show that it has already taken place. Speculation moved increasingly in a Gnostic direction. The Church, which ought to have maintained its unity as *corpus mixtum*, is split up by a latent and often extreme Platonism.

The Church is never triumphant ; it is only militant, i.e., under hostile pressure. A triumphant Church would be the kingdom of God, and no longer ἐκκλησία. Nor is the Assembly of God in Christ to be described as on the one hand visible and on the other invisible. The Christian community in any particular place represents the whole body, and is precisely as visible and temporal as the Christian man. Righteousness and holiness are imputed to the community and to the individual without implying that either of them actually possesses these qualities ; the Church, like the man who is " called ", receives justification and sanctification. If Luther distinguished—above all in his polemic against Rome—between the Church invisible and the Church visible, he was not thereby subscribing to the Platonism of those who came after him. In his translation of the Bible, he does not speak of the Church, but of the congregation of the saints, as the people of God (*qᵉhal Yahwe*) ; and this proves that it is the visible ἐκκλησία, and no essentially invisible Platonic community, which is the object of faith. When Luther goes back to the Old Testament, he is following the

example of Paul.[1] The significance of the primitive
Christian community was recognised by Paul, and
can never lose its importance as the invincible bulwark
against all irresponsible speculations concerning the
Church.[2]

[1] R. Sohm's assertion and inference are characteristic, in
Kirchenrecht II (1923), p. 135 : " The early Church had not yet
attained to the knowledge that the people of God is invisible. In
this way it became catholic. But Luther's discovery that the
Church is invisible spelt the end of Catholicism." The judgment
of Kattenbusch, in the K. Müller Festgabe (1922), must be upheld
against these false notions, when he says that Paul " remains far
superior to all who teach about the Church, including Luther ".

On the controversy over the Church " visible " and " invisible ",
cf. K. L. Schmidt, " Kirchenleitung und Kirchenlehre im N.T. "
in Christentum und Wissenschaft, 8 (1932), 241 ff., esp. 254 ff.
against E. Foerster, " Kirche wider Kirche ", Theol. Rundsch.
(1932), 155 f. C. H. Dodd, in Essays Congregational and Catholic
(1931), deals with the whole question of the Church from the
beginning in relation to the present ecclesiastical situation, and
rightly avoids the distinction between " visible " and " invisible ",
which has spread so widely and done so much harm among the
Churches of the Reformation. It should be noted that Luther himself equated the *ecclesia invisibilis* with the *ecclesia (spiritualis) sola
fide perceptibilis* (see Weimar Ausg. VII, 710—the oldest passage).
J. Boni's treatment of the subject is quite different in Der Kampf
um die Kirche, Studien zum Kirchenbegriff des christlichen
Altertums (1934), p. 130 : " When one reads about the Church in
the N.T., one gets the impression that it is speaking only of an invisible Church ". (Boni's book—326 pages long—is the latest and
most comprehensive treatment of the idea of the Church, and
is the work of a former Swiss Catholic priest, who is now an
evangelical minister. He is not so much concerned with furthering the scientific study of the problems involved as with presenting
a statement of accounts and showing how, as the result of many
years' reading, he developed from a traditionalist conservative
into a modernist liberal.)

[2] Cf. A. Schlatter, " Die Kirche Jerusalems vom Jahre 70-130 ",
in Beitr. Ford. Chr. Th. (1898), 90 : " When Israel died, the
primitive Church also died, and her death became a disaster to
the whole Church ; for the gap was filled by the Christianity of
sects—there Mohammed, here bishop, monk and pope." In spite

As the Church of the N.T. cannot be explained by playing off idea against reality, so also it cannot be explained by playing off the Church as the whole body of believers against the individual congregation. The theological and sociological questions involved are secondary. Every true congregation of the primi-

of its queerness, that is a true saying—true and important in spite of E. Peterson ! The latter rightly observes, in Die Kirche (1929), p. 69, " If anyone sees the relation of the Church to the Synagogue as merely a historical, and not as a theological problem, he is bound to revive the Gnostic standpoint, and seek the elimination of the O.T. and of the Messiah according to the flesh. Thus it is no accident that Harnack the historian was sympathetic to the theology of Marcion the Gnostic." But it is not quite clear what he sees when he says, speaking as a theologian, that the Church Fathers, in contrast to the Synagogue, understood *ecclesia* to mean ἐκκαλεῖν, *evocatio*, a calling out of the world, with its natural ordinances and natural sociological creations (pp. 24 ff.), and when he writes as follows : " Cf. also C. Passaglia, De Ecclesia Christi, I (1853), p. 10—I hold this patristic interpretation of the word ἐκκλησία, which helps to differentiate between the constitutional forms of Ekklesia and Synagoge to be more significant than modern demonstrations that ἐκκλησία and συναγωγή are used promiscuously in the LXX. The true meaning of a word is not settled by a quotation, but by the concrete situation in which it is uttered " (p. 70). But more than mere " quotation " is involved in the relation between O.T. and N.T. And to talk about the " concrete situation " smacks more of history than of theology. Peterson has combined his three Salzburg lectures on " die Kirche aus Juden und Heiden " in Schweiz. Rundsch. (Jan. 1936), 875 ff., and while the article is helpful in its survey of the relations between Church and Synagogue, its conclusions are not altogether clear. In the N.T., at any rate, ἐκκλησία and συναγωγή are not so sharply differentiated as Peterson urges. The Church Fathers whom he follows, in conscious agreement with old Christian and mediaeval methods of Biblical interpretation, relying on Romans ix-xi, regarded ἐκκλησία as the true (spiritual) Israel, and συναγωγή as the false (after the flesh), and this has finally become stereotyped, though it could not be the intention of the N.T. as a whole. (See p. 33.)

tive Church represented the whole body as really
as the congregation at Jerusalem. The gradual
drawing together of many congregations in one
organisation naturally suggests a development from
individual to corporate. But this impression is misleading, since the only criterion of genuineness is to
be found in the congregation's conviction that it
represents the whole body. The much discussed controversial question about what is called the development
of a system of Church government should be tackled
from this point of view. Self-evident matters of
constitution are hardly worth our attention. The N.T.
shows very clearly that in the beginning there was
more leadership by men of the Spirit (Pneumatikertum
und Charismatikertum) than in later days, and that
their place was afterwards taken by presbyters and
bishops. But the way in which Paul thinks and
speaks about the gifts of the spirit (χαρίσματα), and
particularly the way in which he maintains connection
with the original group of believers, shows that it is not
legitimate to speak of an essential constitutional change
from a " pneumatic " to a " juristic " form. When
the time did come, in which matters of human law were
given the status of matters of divine law—a change that
was largely made possible by the " high " speculations
about the ἐκκλησία—then the step was taken from
original Christianity to early Catholicism, a step which,
rightly understood, marks the cleavage between
Protestantism and Catholicism.

6

INDEX OF WORDS AND REFERENCES

74 INDEX

PAGE